Reporter Richard Ostling's significant first book weaves personal anecdotes, material from confidential sources, solid historical research, and careful investigation of current church theory and practice into a convincing case for freedom of information in the churches. Ostling's main target is the Roman Catholic church but his aim takes in Protestant churches too. Despite a subtle difference in style, both Protestants and Catholics have their well-guarded secrets. As Ostling puts it, "When a mainstream Protestant bureaucrat is found practicing secrecy, it is with a sheepish grin on his face, rather than with the righteous visage of the secretive Catholic prelate."

Just how entrenched is secrecy in church policy? Ostling first surveys the current scene in the broader context of recent secular disputes over secrecy in government. The ploys, diversions, and tactics of recent administrations—and the response of the public and the media to them—are not dissimilar from those of the Vatican and the U.S. hierarchy. The issue raised is the constituent's right to know what affects his life, whether it involves campaign financing or church contributions, which Ostling calls "God's mammon." Despite recent policy changes, the Catholic church hedges on the issue, as a number of revealing, humorous, damaging instances show only too well.

(continued on back flap)

(continued from front flap)

Even today there are bulwarks against opening up the church: the present Code of Canon Law, the closed-door regulations of the Vatican Archives, and the Vatican's theological watchdog agency, the Congregation for the Doctrine of the Faith. But there is also a tradition of secrecy which goes back to the beginnings of the church. Or does it? Here Ostling unearths some surprising facts from history, showing that many secrecy practices resulted from the peculiar hostilities of the last century. Nor should appeal be made to the "right to privacy" where administrative, and not personal, matters are at stake.

The case for candor in the church, then, is a strong one, and Ostling makes his point even stronger in the final chapters of the book. On the basis of democratic principles and recent theological discussion, he argues for free access to information on a "right-to-know" rather than a "need-to-know" basis. The church is clearly not exempt from this responsibility to its membership and to the public in general. It may continue to draw the curtain and hide behind closed doors, but it does so at the risk of its own integrity and credibility in an increasingly skeptical age.

SECRECY IN THE CHURCH thus adds an important note to post-Vatican II church-reform literature. Ostling touches a question that is vital to church members and leaders alike and demands the kind of sensible and realistic answer that he gives it.

SECRECY
IN
THE CHURCH

SECRECY IN THE CHURCH

A Reporter's Case
for the
Christian's Right to Know

Richard N. Ostling

HARPER & ROW, PUBLISHERS

NEW YORK, EVANSTON, SAN FRANCISCO, LONDON

FIRST EDITION

Designed by Gwendolyn O. England

Library of Congress Cataloging in Publication Data

Ostling, Richard N
  Secrecy in the church.
  Bibliography: p.
  1. Freedom of information in the church.
2. Catholic Church—Government. I. Title.
BV740.086   262′.3   73–18701
ISBN 0–06–066395–2

1795725

Contents

Part I

THE SECRECY SCENE

1 "Nothing Hidden"

One day after he had been teaching a huge throng along the shore of the Sea of Galilee, Jesus got into an after-hours discussion with his dozen disciples. They found it hard to understand what he had been talking about, which means the crowd must have been even more confused. So Jesus began explaining the parables to the Twelve, and in doing so he added a new one. If you have a lamp, he asked, do you conceal it under a basket or under your bed? No, you put it on a lampstand. Then he drove his point home:

"There is nothing hidden but it must be disclosed; nothing kept secret except to be brought to light."

The Parable of the Lamp holds true these nineteen centuries later. During the period in which this book was written, things hidden were being disclosed with stunning regularity in the cluster of scandals known as "Watergate." This and other controversies of the 1970s have raised unprecedented issues about the control of information that will be discussed by the ethics experts long after the courts have ruled and the names and dates from a thousand newspaper articles and a hundred days of TV hearings have blurred in memory. A sampling:

Is secrecy in "national security" information so important that the government is justified in invading the privacy of high officials and newsmen by wiretaps to see if they are involved in "leaks"?

Was Daniel Ellsberg a hero or a knave for breaking the secrecy canons of his job and leaking the "Pentagon Papers" so the public could learn this information about Vietnam? Did the leak actually harm national security? Did the Papers contain such essential data, not available otherwise, that the press had a responsibility to print them?

Did national security warrant false statements and concealment of information about 3,630 bombing missions over Cambodia and guerrilla operations in Laos?

Is the need for confidentiality of information within the White House so pressing that a President should seek to deny prosecutors, courts, and Congress access to tape recordings which contain possible evidence of crimes?

Did the telecasts of the Senate Watergate hearings spread unfair information about innocent persons and did they make unbiased trials impossible? Even if they did, were they justifiable in order to inform the public?

Was the U.S. Supreme Court correct to deny a special "privilege" for investigative reporters who want to protect their confidential sources of information? Are reporters right to go to jail rather than break secrecy promises to these sources, even when information about crimes is involved?

Should columnist Jack Anderson have published top-secret memos about Administration maneuvers in the India-Pakistan war so soon after the events, thus embarrassing the U.S. government? Or the opposite—should Anderson have bowed to a judge's request to stop printing data from the secret proceedings of the Watergate grand jury?

Speaking of grand juries, was then-Vice President Spiro Agnew correct to protest about news leaks of the investigation of graft charges against him even before the grand jury had heard the evidence? Or were the allegations so important that the public had a right to know about them before they went through channels?

For those interested in less cosmic questions, was a judge justified to side with the heirs of Warren G. Harding and halt publication of the President's love letters to his mistress until the twenty-first century? A major defeat for the growing Peephole School of historians.

These questions are not just a game journalists and politicians play, nor a twentieth-century equivalent of "how many angels can stand on the head of a pin?" Since knowledge is power, each of these cases is a parable of power, the power of access to useful information. The U.S. Congress complains that its constitutional power to control spending, declare war, and approve treaties has been thwarted by secrecy in the executive branch. Citizenship in a democracy means little without information. Even totalitarian governments are accountable to their people, and the degree of accountability increases with the degree of democracy. A citizen (or subject) can have little involvement with his government apart from reliable information about it. The news media figure in these disputes, because they are the only source of information for most people.

Freedom of information has been built into the democratic political theory of the West. In the eighteenth century James Madison provided a succinct American statement of this assumption: "A popular government without popular information or the means of acquiring it is but a prologue to a farce or a tragedy, or perhaps both. . . . The right of freely examining public characters and measures, and of free communication thereon, is the only effectual guardian of every other right."

What holds for government also applies to other institutions that have profound effects in modern society. Certainly Christianity, with its millions of members and dollars, is such an institution. The Christian church has a special claim to be the champion of truth, and truth is without value if no one knows it. In the first instance the church has a responsibility to its own constituency. There are also reasons why the world outside the church membership has a right to church information. To give a simple example, public schools need to know how many children plan to attend parochial schools. Beyond that a church which benefits from the society has responsibilities to it; indeed some Catholics now reason that tax exemption and other traditional privileges create an obligation to open up church finances.

Sometimes church secrecy has the air of urbanity of an East Coast Episcopal bishop. Sometimes it has the rugged prairie individualism of a broadcast evangelist, who refuses to improve his public image by opening his multi-million-dollar books. In the Roman Catholic church secrecy is often medieval, with solemn pledges, double-locked doors, and paid informants sneaking secrets out of the fortress. And sometimes it gets plain ridiculous, with reporters from major newspapers lying on the floor behind a piano to eavesdrop on secret meetings of bishops, or Vatican correspondents devising ways to circumvent the secrecy system and ending up reporting the death of two popes by mistake.

Secrecy as an issue is brand-new in Catholicism. Even a few years ago it was so widely practiced that hardly anyone even mentioned it except a few disgruntled reporters. But the case for freedom of information is compelling, and the right to know is of growing importance among the church's vast membership. After the development of an entrenched culture of secrecy, which this book will survey, Catholicism is beginning to change, in this as in so many other things. The purpose of focusing on the Catholic church is to study the largest, and one of the most secretive, branches of Christianity. Before the case for candor is completed, Protestant secrecy will also receive some scrutiny.

Freedom of information is part of democratic theory, and the Catholic church makes no claims to being a democracy. Even so, it has a vital stake in this freedom. For one thing, there is a strong Christian tradition in favor of open information. For another, Catholic philosophy traditionally puts great confidence in the reason of the individual human being, and a closed-door culture is an admission that church leaders look upon Christians as children rather than as fully responsible members of the body of Christ. The Christian view of man had a major influence on the development of Western democratic theory, and democracy is now influencing Catholic thought.

On a less idealistic plane, secrecy is less desirable, and far less feasible, than in the days when Mother Church was obeyed without question. The internal affairs of Catholicism have been changed irrevocably since Vatican Council II. U.S. Catholics are also influenced by the culture around them. Americans have always scrutinized authorities and institutions, but in an eerie way that defies satisfactory analysis most institutions are on the defensive today as never before. Each is expected to reexamine itself and to justify its ways. Even before Watergate came along, the Vietnam War had shattered many assumptions about the way America operates. The signs of change abound: consumers and citizens feel betrayed by many practices of big business, its often-secret influence on government, its emphasis on development at the expense of environment. Nader's Raiders have expanded from business to poking into politics; politicians are expected to reveal where their campaign contributions really come from. The youth, Black, and women's movements may not be able to sustain a "new politics," but they have wrought change throughout the society.

The secular culture may become more open, or more secretive, and thus affect the church, but the church must first of all be true to itself, to its own teachings and traditions. Basically, this book is about these teachings and traditions. Though the case is made by a reporter who covers religion, the issue transcends the mere convenience of newsmen. The book is an attempt to examine the theology of candor from within the context of Catholic history and belief.

What arguments generally have been used to justify secrecy in human affairs, and how have they been answered by the advocates of openness? Obviously there are sometimes good reasons to use secrecy in any kind of organization. Even newsmen recognize this, and indeed they claim secrecy for themselves when their confidential sources must be protected. In government as well as in church the need for confidential discussions during the formulation of policy is one of the most persuasive arguments. This was the reason that, in a sense, the United States of America was born in secrecy. At the Constitutional Convention of 1787 participants were sworn to secrecy, and historians speculate that if the sessions had been open at the time, the significant compromises might not have been achieved. It is worth noting, however, that the most eminent of the Founding Fathers who was not a member of the Convention, Thomas Jefferson, opposed the policy. With the broad extension of public participation in American government since that time it is doubtful that such a meeting would be held in tight secrecy today.

Modern-day examples of secrecy in the formulation of government policy are the much-debated "executive privilege" in the White House and the federal departments, the closed-door deliberations of the U.S. Supreme Court, and the secrecy in some of the committee meetings where the Congress does much of its legislative work. The House of Representatives decided in 1973 to put the burden of proof on those who want secret committee meetings, especially the "mark-up" sessions where bills are voted on section by section. The Senate still holds to its musty traditions.

The Catholic equivalent of this is the secret policy-making that remains customary in diocesan chancery offices, national bishops' conferences (with the recent exception of the U.S.), and the Vatican Curia. The "advisory" councils on the local and national levels, and the world bishops' synod which advises the pope, have not loosened this situation to any major degree.

A related matter is secrecy in diplomacy. In the idealistic Wilsonian era after World War I many political scientists believed that the war had been caused largely by excessive secrecy in foreign affairs. The popular slogan of that day was "open agreements, openly arrived at." In the practical world of politics a more reasonable slogan would be "open agreements, openly arrived at, after secret consultations."

After Jack Anderson printed the secret memos about U.S. policy toward Pakistan and India, the *New York Times'* James Reston wrote that modern photocopying was having a dangerous impact. With memos reproduced and leaking all over, foreign envoys who once could send their disagreements with national policy back home over a private pipeline now face the risk that their candid comments may be circulated. In this strange way, Reston said, the copying machines that were intended to expand truth and information are, instead, inhibiting honest discussion and dissent in the formulation of foreign policy.

As befits a national institution, the *Times* itself has played a role in the art of diplomatic secrecy. In 1961 the newspaper bowed to pressure from President Kennedy and did not print details it had learned about the projected Bay of Pigs invasion of Cuba. Later both Kennedy and the editors regretted the deal, because the nation would have been better off if publicity had aborted the escapade. During the Cuban missile crisis Kennedy also asked the *Times* to withhold for one day the information it had acquired about U.S. knowledge of the Soviet installations in Cuba. The newspaper agreed after Kennedy vowed that he would not start a war during the period of the blackout. Max Frankel, then of the *Times* Washington bureau, says the arrangement was based upon mutual trust, something which had vanished by the time the Vietnam War began mushrooming.

The Roman Catholic church, of course, has its own diplomatic corps operating out of the mini-state of Vatican City, and it generally operates with a high degree of secrecy in its dealings with various regimes. In the case of delicate negotiations with Communist governments the secrecy is certainly understandable. Catholic officialdom also uses vast amounts of secrecy in the internal diplomacy which is necessary in running a giant church.

By far the most emotional justification for secrecy is "national security." Most thoughtful people, including journalists, grant the need for secrecy in legitimate cases of overriding national interest, but the case has been made suspect by the promiscuous use of the executive cover-up and of the classification stamp. Bureaucrats have been known to "classify" menus for state dinners and newspaper clippings. (When the *New York Times* once went on strike, the C.I.A.'s daily classified intelligence report to federal agencies suddenly shrank to half its normal size.) Wide-scale secrecy began with the Cold War, and unfortunately the shift to a Tepid War has not changed the practice. A House report put the cost of federal secret-keeping at $60 million to $80 million a year, and the experts say the volume of data which is classified far exceeds the amount readily available to the public.

Washington reporters know that secrecy-minded officials almost routinely leak information—when it serves their purpose. Historian Theodore Draper was irritated when a backer of the U.S. intervention in the Dominican Republic got access to secret files for a scholarly attack on Draper's criticism of it. Draper wrote that the classification system is "shot through with duplicity, hypocrisy, and favoritism." Insiders, even Presidents, violate the code "with impunity and often for profit." Similar calculated leaks have long been used by officials in the Catholic church to further the causes they support.

The Vietnam War has given secrecy a bad name in the United States. The Pentagon Papers were important chiefly because they showed a government that misled its citizens by withholding information. As Arthur Schlesinger, Jr., once remarked, the system "has kept more things from the American people than it has from the enemy." The Communists in Southeast Asia, China, and the Soviet Union knew all about the secret bombing and guerrilla warfare—only the Congress and the taxpayers were ignorant. (In the case of those 3,630 secret bombing missions even the Secretary of the Air Force was not entrusted with knowledge of what his squads were doing.)

Because the Ellsberg case was dismissed for government improprieties, the nation was deprived of a dramatic judicial test on national security. The Espionage Act, written during World War I and revised in 1950, prohibits disclosure of information "relating to the national defense." Ellsberg was the first nonspy to be prosecuted under the act. He had no intention of harming the U.S., and was accused, not of handing data to the Russians, but to the American people. Interestingly, it was not a crime as such for Ellsberg to flaunt the "Top Secret" stamp that was put routinely on the Pentagon Papers. An official who leaks classified documents can be reprimanded, or fired, but cannot be charged with a crime. To do that, wrote David Wise in *The Politics of Lying* (1973), "would be an invitation and a license for government to classify anything and everything it pleased. Under such a system the government's control over information would be total." After the Ellsberg trial President Nixon asked for just such a change, under which leaks would be criminal regardless of whether there was any actual harm to security.

(In Great Britain the Official Secrets Act of 1911 forbids communication of information by a government official or contractor to any unauthorized person, and makes the recipient of the information equally guilty. The London *Sunday Telegraph* was prosecuted for printing criticisms of the Nigerian army from a report by a British military adviser who had given the report to the newspaper himself. The *Telegraph* was acquitted in 1971.)

A further ethical question about Ellsberg is whether the supplying of these documents to the newspapers constituted theft. Moral theology has always condoned theft in extreme circumstances, e.g., stealing bread to feed starving children. It could be argued that Vietnam constituted a similar emergency, since it was also a matter of life and death, if the release of the Papers would have had a crucial effect and if the war was "unjust."

A rough Catholic parallel to the Pentagon Papers was enacted in 1967 when a member of Pope Paul's top-secret advisory commission on birth control leaked the majority report which favored a liberalized teaching. The pope eventually overruled his advisers, and knowledge of the weight of scholarly Catholic opinion on the other side contributed to the major erosion of papal authority in the wake of Paul's encyclical. An ecclesiastical Daniel Ellsberg had decided that a transcendent moral concern justified the breaking of his bonds of secrecy, and America's *National Catholic Reporter* and *Le Monde* of Paris filled the *New York Times*' Pentagon Papers role in releasing the document.

Because the public is so dependent on the press for information, it is important to realize that the performance of journalists is as much a reminder of man's fallen nature as is the performance of bishops and bureaucrats. Walter Lippmann's prescient 1922 book, *Public Opinion,* said that the citizen should ask himself how close he really is to the facts. "Who actually saw, heard, felt, counted, named the thing about which you have an opinion? Was it the man who told you, or the man who told him, or someone still further removed?" Besides these barriers of access, the quality of journalistic information can be hindered by honest mistakes, by lack of skill, or by conscious distortion by the reporter. The speed that is essential to the enterprise increases the difficulties.

The press can also be a willing or unwitting partner in cases where publicity is as much a form of political coercion as secrecy is, for instance in the ballyhooing of charges made by the late Senator Joseph McCarthy. Freedom of information and freedom of the press do not always guarantee positive results. Intelligent citizens should keep the journalists, as well as the officeholders, under scrutiny, but with the same basic trust that is necessary for either to function. The solution to these defects is not more restrictions on the media, but better journalism.

What of the opposite side, the case for candor? There is surprisingly little past wisdom to draw upon, probably because freedom of information is so fundamental to our system that it has hardly been noticed. One might start with the landmark report in 1947 by the Commission on the Freedom of the Press (which included W. E. Hocking, Reinhold Niebuhr, and Jacques Maritain as a foreign adviser). The commission obviously supported the right of the public to information, but it never really made a case for it. At the time, the commission was more concerned with its notion that government meddling would help improve American journalism—which in retrospect can only be termed bizarre.

Most newsmen, whether they cover church or state, have good reason to believe that all too often secrecy amounts to simple self-protection by institutions or officials without any ethical basis. The dangers are acute when the officials themselves have the power to decide whether the secrecy is justified. In the U.S. federal system, at least in theory, the potential abuse of misguided policies and errant officials is mitigated by the power of the three branches of government to monitor one another. In the Catholic church the effective executive, legislative, and judicial power is held by the same group of officials, so there is no such check. Secrecy is particularly tempting to officials during times of ferment, which adds to the possibilities of misuse in Catholicism today.

Several books and essays have offered solid common-sense arguments against secrecy in a democracy, particularly *Freedom or Secrecy* (1964) by James Russell Wiggins, the former managing editor of the *Washington Post*. Their case can be summarized as follows:

1. Secrecy is based upon a low opinion of the public, and ultimately of the individual man. The power of democratic government resides with the whole people and is merely yielded to representatives acting for the whole; information is the essential link between them.

2. Secrecy is impossible. Information will get out eventually, so the choice is between a timely, full, accurate, honest, useful report available to everyone; and a distorted, inaccurate hearsay account which gets to some people much earlier than others. (One proponent of this Sieve Theory is John Kenneth Galbraith, who says there is a rule in Washington which is totally without exceptions: "Nothing of civil import remains a secret, and certainly not if it is shared by more than two people." Even conservative nuclear physicist Edward Teller thinks atomic secrets should be classified for only one year and then

made public, because "if the Russians really want to find out, they can find it in one year.")

3. Secrecy generates mutual suspicions, adds to the distance, and destroys the confidence between people and their government. It also limits the possibilities of public good will in implementing a program once it has been approved.

4. Secrecy prevents the education of citizens, and also eliminates the valuable input that an informed public can add during the formulation of a program.

5. Secrecy removes an important check upon the conduct of officials, and encourages deception and out-and-out wrongdoing in office. On the other hand, secrecy also limits the protection of an honest official from false accusations. In a democracy purges should be carried out in the polling booth and the courtroom.

6. Secrecy gives advantages of information to a select elite, e.g., highly profitable knowledge about stocks, taxes, and future economic events.

Wiggins adds, "The consequences of secrecy are not less because the reasons for secrecy are more. The ill effects are the same whether the reasons for secrecy are good or bad."

Except perhaps for the last point, one can simply insert the appropriate ecclesiastical nouns and the arguments hold equally well within the church. Even with the first point, admitting that bishops are not democratic "representatives," the leaders of the church are still accountable to their members, and the low opinion of man violates Catholic as well as democratic philosophy. Generally speaking, secrecy operates with considerable similarity in government and in the church, which should not be surprising since both are human communities. However, before considering in detail how much of the democratic case against secrecy applies to the church, we will see how the phenomenon has appeared in recent times, and how it developed historically. And what more appropriate place to look first than the nerve center of Catholicism, the Vatican?

2 Secrecy—Vatican Style

There is something quaintly symbolic about the way the Roman Catholic church announces to the world the end of a ballot inside the secret conclaves where the cardinals elect a new pope. Smoke signals —the most primitive form of communication known to man. A blast of black smoke means the ballot did not break the deadlock; white smoke means the church has its new leader. But the archaic system sometimes fails to communicate. The smoky chaos of 1958 was described by the Associated Press bureau chief in Rome, Allan Jacks. The second smoke cloud looked white and the Vatican Radio's priestly announcer proclaimed, "We have a new pope!" Secular newsmen jumped, but it turned out that the Vatican Radio man had no inside track; he was just another smoke watcher. The smoke turned gray, then black. At that point savvy reporters gave up on the smoke game and the radio and looked for other telltale signs: formation of the Swiss Guards and the Vatican band.

The smoke system may be inefficient, but at least it has some charm, a quality entirely lacking in other instances of Vatican failure to communicate. The Vatican, and the church generally, is caught in ambivalence on the important question of freedom of information. Official statements have recognized the people's right to know, and relations with newsmen have improved greatly in the era of Vatican Council II. And yet secrecy is still widespread. The problem is par-

15

ticularly acute at the Vatican, which still has much of the atmosphere of the medieval court that it once was. Vatican officials quite naturally identify the press in general with the pecularities of periodicals that they see in Italy, with their sensationalism, anticlericalism, and a bizarre news sense that has produced those *paparazzi* (photographers) who pursue the famous like a swarm of wasps. The Vatican is also influenced by an Italian culture that lacks the long tradition of the people's right to know which exists in American political theory.

For almost all of its history the Vatican has had no formal policy at all on information, but just an unexpressed assumption that most matters should never be made public. That is the conclusion of John A. Lee, a priest who did one of the first intensive studies of Vatican communications for his Ph.D. dissertation at the University of Minnesota. Put more bluntly, the public relations program of an institution governing 650 million souls has been based largely on unexamined tradition and caprice. It was not until 1973 that the Vatican made available for public purchase something so basic as a complete statistical survey on membership, parishes, priests, and members of religious orders.

The phenomenon of a group of newsmen regularly covering the Vatican is a relatively new development. As recently as a half-century ago, when the pope was still a sequestered "prisoner of the Vatican," few papers except Catholic ones carried much Vatican news. Even *L'Osservatore Romano,* the Vatican's own newspaper, did not report the pope's speeches directly until 1927. Up to the late 1940s the source of much of the information that leaked out was a colorful monsignor named Enrico Pucci. Pucci, a longtime correspondent for America's National Catholic News Service, filled the vacuum left by the lack of a regular source for official information. He got material from his friends in the Curia and fed it to secular newsmen. It was not always accurate, but at least it gave the frustrated reporters something to start with. In one famous yarn, Pucci managed to sell three news agencies three totally different "inside" stories about the

terms Italy planned to grant the Vatican under the Lateran Treaty.
The most outlandish tipster was Virgilio Scattolini, who was fired
by *L'Osservatore Romano* in 1939 and began writing an anonymous,
confidential bulletin on Vatican events. According to Robert A. Graham, a Jesuit expert on Vatican diplomatic history, "Scattolini in-
vented everything. He was never known to furnish any real news." He
would take an actual event, such as a private papal audience, and then
apply his imagination to it to concoct supposed inside dope. His
phony stories were taken seriously by American, German, and Soviet
intelligence during World War II, and many were splashed worldwide
by major wire services and newspapers. Finally, he was arrested in
1948 and sentenced to six months in jail for "acts hostile to a foreign
state" because of his fabrication of Vatican news. The Scattolini scandal shows the dangers of the sort of rumor market that existed when
reliable Vatican information was so inaccessible, but Graham insists
that it also proves the laziness and gullibility of newsmen.

Barrett McGurn recalls that when he first went to Rome for the
New York Herald Tribune in 1939, one news agency had to cover the
pope's speeches by having two Italian stenographers type out the
words as they came over Vatican Radio, which led to many inaccura-
cies. Not until the 1950s could reporters get official texts at the moment the pope spoke, or sometimes shortly before. But even this
provided little time to work through the theological thicket and ex-
tract the news.

McGurn said in *A Reporter Looks at the Vatican* (1962) that the
Vatican had "incredibly poor press relations." For many years there
was no press office at all, and no authorized spokesman to whom
reporters could go with questions. After much pressure the Vatican
finally set up a press office, but it was twice removed from the sources.
It was not a Vatican office at all, but a press office at *L'Osservatore
Romano,* which is technically a "semi-official" newspaper. The
spokesman there often knew nothing, and when he did he was afraid
to comment or else said he could reveal nothing because of the secrecy

rules. The office was not manned in the afternoon or evening, it held no press conferences to provide background on papal statements, never tipped reporters when a major statement was expected, and could not even get reporters decent seats at public functions.

For these reasons the secular press corps was forced to develop a network of tipsters within the Vatican. For many years Vatican coverage necessitated a level of bribery and information-purchasing which was probably unprecedented in modern journalism. One veteran of the Rome coverage in the 1950s says "there was nothing like it in any other nation, where there was no way to get the information except to buy it." McGurn says that the low-paid Vatican staffers were offered "tips, salaries, outright bribes, and ingenious sales talks." A printer at *L'Osservatore* used to sell the list of bishop appointments in advance until, as legend has it, he was trapped when officials planted a false name. Another Vatican layman with access to papal statements used to leak them several hours before the official release time—even though the actual speech had already been delivered.

The head of one American bureau in Rome in the 1950s recalls that his three or four tipsters cost about $80 a month, but when the pope was ill or something else out of the ordinary developed, the expenses would rise to several hundred dollars a month. This bureau chief says he never bought anything directly from clergymen in the Vatican, and never knew whether his lay intermediaries were passing on part of their payment or not. Some tipsters worked on retainer, others by "piecework." Did this newsman worry about the ethics of all this? "It was really scandalous. It was their system and I hated it, but you simply had to do it. I had no compunction about it, because my job was to find out what was happening. We very seldom could get interviews, even to have someone provide us some guidance. The Vatican wouldn't tip us officially on an announcement. And when the pope got sick the press office would only say that he was 'indisposed.' So on top of our regular payroll, we had to lay out more hundreds among the entourage of the papal doctors."

The worst part of it was that the various newsmen were forever sending out conflicting stories. In an article for *Life* upon the death of Pope Pius XII, Emmet John Hughes, the chief foreign correspondent for Time Incorporated, complained:

> The press office of the Vatican, the only official source of the world's news of the Papacy, could perhaps be forgiven its inefficiency but not its corruption. Here underlings release, invent and sell 'news' with callous and candid calculation and abandon. The dishonor and the scandal that they invite are scarcely more remarkable than the looseness of organization that has permitted such a condition to exist without their superiors being aware of it.

Along with the tipsters, of course, the Vatican reporters depended on calculated official leaks by the Vatican, or by one of the factions within the Vatican.

Secrecy plagued the contingent of reporters who were assigned to the death watch for Pope Pius XII in 1958. The official medical bulletins were contradictory, overoptimistic, and vague, and reporters were barred from the grounds of the papal palace. Dependent as usual on emergency measures, one Italian news agency made a deal with an employee to signal by opening a particular window in the palace when the pope died. Someone else in search of fresh air opened the window by mistake, and Rome newspapers rushed out extras reporting—two days early—"The Pope Is Dead!" The press also had to fuss and fume just to get inside St. Peter's for the funeral.

The late Harold Schachern of the *Detroit News,* a Catholic layman, said that during the entire period not a single word in English, either spoken or written, was available in the press office. The facilities for the throng of reporters consisted of two tables, two phones, and three battered typewriters—with European keyboards. When Pope John XXIII was dying in 1963, the splendid press room that had been initiated for Vatican Council II was chained and padlocked. One day Schachern was chatting with a group of Vatican correspondents which included veterans of such assignments as the Kremlin and the

Korean War. They all agreed that "the toughest, most demanding, and certainly the most frustrating assignment in all of journalism's history was the pre-conciliar Vatican," Schachern recalled in an article for *Ave Maria.*

Even with the improvements during and since Vatican II, experienced reporters estimate that only one-fifth of their information comes from official sources. *Time's* Vatican correspondent, Wilton Wynn, remarks that "everything depends on personal contacts based on friendship and mutual trust." He has learned that the various major Vatican offices ("congregations") operate so independently that when something important breaks within one Vatican circle it is usually a secret to the other Vatican departments. These days, despite the continuing official pledges to secrecy, Wynn says an experienced reporter can find people in the bureaucracy willing to talk on all sides of any issue—so long as they are not quoted by name. As Wynn sees it, the Vatican has the worst of both worlds. The secrecy system is not working, so it is of no value. But since the Vatican refuses to drop its official commitment to secrecy, it tarnishes its image in the modern world.

What if they gave an ecumenical council and nobody came? Odd as it seems, the Catholic church acted as though it could assemble 2,500 prelates from around the world for Vatican II, the first council in nearly a century, without attracting much press attention. As it happened, the council sometimes drew more than 1,000 reporters. The First Session of 1962, the only one presided over by John XXIII, had a rather disastrous public relations policy. The bishops were dissatisfied because of all the rumors, speculation, and misinformed reporting. For their part, the reporters were angered by the dearth of trustworthy information and the lack of cooperation from officials.

Robert Kaiser, who covered Vatican II for *Time,* provides many detailed complaints about the First Session in *Pope, Council and World* (1963). He says that before the council, Pope John had set up the first official press office in Vatican history. But it was headed by

Monsignor Fausto Vaillainc who, Kaiser says, put out "smoke screens of inconsequential fact intended to camouflage the event." The office's policies "bespoke a contempt for the world's press and the public it represented," and were an "insult to the Council Fathers." Vaillainc wrote a journalist several months before the council, "We do not need the press." The Vatican required reporters to provide evidence of a "proper spirit of reverence" to get press credentials, then lost many of the applications.

Monsignor John E. Kelly, the information director for the U.S. bishops, saw it coming. He worked out a detailed plan to assist newsmen who would inevitably face obstacles when they arrived at the Vatican. But the American hierarchy was still suspicious of the press in 1962 and Kelly's plans were rejected. Since the meetings were to be secret under the official rules, the bishops saw little sense in accommodating newsmen. Gerald Renner, who had been Kelly's assistant, explains: "The American bishops failed to sense on the eve of the council the intensity of interest, or to even glimpse its potential consequences for the future of the church. Conditioned by the doctrine of papal infallibility proclaimed at Vatican I, and lulled by the lackluster sessions that they themselves engaged in, the U.S. bishops trooped off to Rome more to get their marching orders than to participate forcefully in setting new directions for the church." Since the bishops had rejected his basic proposals for handling the biggest story in his career, Kelly quit. Not with a meek letter, but with the fanfare of a Washington press conference. He then went into exile, as a parish pastor in a small New Jersey town, where he died in obscurity in 1970.

Yet the American bishops learned quickly. By the end of the First Session they had put all of his ideas into operation: daily news briefings, panels of bishops and *periti* ("experts") to provide necessary background, a documentation service, and liaison personnel. Other national groups of bishops, and the Divine Word order, also set up information channels around the Vatican's official office. One reason for the opening up, undoubtedly, was that enterprising reporters were getting the news anyway. Several of the top European dailies filled the role of a daily bulletin, while Kaiser in *Time* and the anonymous "Xavier Rynne" team of the *New Yorker* provided the inside story for the American audience. One archbishop said, "I thought I'd be pursued by reporters seeking information. Now I find that I'm pursuing the reporters to try to find out what the devil is going on."

The late Edward L. Heston, who later became an archbishop and head of the Vatican communications secretariat, recalled that on the opening day of the council reporters got a verbal briefing, but the briefing officers were not authorized even to sit in the sessions at St. Peter's. So Heston and the other spokesmen were forced to use the official bulletin of the council secretariat, described by Heston as "uninformative, jejune, newsless, and noncommittal." "Xavier Rynne" said that these official bulletins seemed to have been written in advance of the discussion, and generally favored the party line of the Vatican Curia. Although names make news, on only one day was the name of a bishop connected with a specific proposal, and this lapse brought the *Dies Irae* upon the press office. When summaries of speeches were available, they were often inadequate because of important last-minute additions on the floor. Frustrated, many papers recalled their correspondents from Rome. U.S. freelancer Paul Brindel solved the problem one day by sneaking past the Swiss Guards and plainclothesmen into the back row of the choir in St. Peter's, wearing a cassock.

Despite grumbling from officials, Heston began offering reporters his own English-language report on developments rather than just translating the official bulletin from the Italian, thus winning the reputation as "the answer to a newsman's prayer." The pressure for bland accounts from spokesmen was strongest, of course, when new opinions or disagreements cropped up—the very thing that creates news. As Heston observed, no measures taken by officialdom could have bottled up the news. Besides that, these conflicts showed the vitality of the church, and were not something to hide in shame. Due to the secrecy rule, bishops and others speaking at the English-language press briefings during the First Session sometimes proved reticent. The spirit of '62 was symbolized when Cardinal Montini of Milan was asked by the press office to release the text of his important speech about the decree on the church. Irritated by Italian newspaper distortion of one of his weekly letters from the council, Montini wrote back, "I cannot provide any information, nor do I think it would really be worthwhile."

No one knows why, but the same man, as the newly elected Pope Paul, directed a renovation in the council's press policy before the Second Session. He appointed a study committee headed by American Archbishop Martin J. O'Connor, then president of the communications office. The result was a turnabout. Heads of the news bureaus handling the various language groups were to sit in St. Peter's, and they were to be provided with all available texts. They were authorized to report everything that was said and done in the council hall. The secrecy obligation was restricted just to meetings of the council commissions, and to texts of documents under discussion. Heston recalled that reporters made *pro forma* protests about not being admitted to St. Peter's themselves, but few would have had the necessary knowledge of Latin, the language on the council floor. As the English officer, Heston was now responsible for a half-hour verbal briefing after each meeting, preparation of a more complete daily bulletin which many of the bishops also found useful, the midafternoon press panels, and special press conferences. As for digging out the behind-the-scenes maneuvering, the reporters were on their own, as they would be at a political convention. The church benefited by the change since, as Kelly's successor Monsignor Vincent Yzermans remarked, "it was not the bishops but the press that made Vatican II the greatest religious event of our times."

The council provided for future meetings of a mini-council, the world Synod of Bishops, a new body of representatives to meet periodically in Rome to advise the pope. At the first synod in 1967 press policy regressed to the level of the council's First Session. Only one press officer was allowed into the secret meetings, and he issued a daily summary of the speeches in Italian. But unlike the later practice at Vatican II, he was told to "scramble" the minutes so reporters could not tell who had said what. Nor could the reporters get a sense of the interplay between speakers, or the context in which comments had been made.

Things were considerably better at the 1969 synod, but the discussion papers were kept secret. Three weeks into that meeting England's John Cardinal Heenan complained that "much confusion and anxiety before the synod could have been avoided by publication of its working papers. Eventually they leaked out, because you can't keep secret anything that is known to 2,000 bishops. The secrecy was needless, and only provided grounds for suspicion and rumor." Despite the improvements at the synod itself, the next month the applications for Vatican press credentials included an ominous warning that a press card might be withdrawn if a reporter showed "an incorrect attitude . . . toward the Church and toward the Holy See."

The old-fashioned spirit still lingered at the October 1971 synod. Pope Paul opened the meeting with a warning to delegates to ignore outside "pressures" from the press and church groups. Meanwhile, the synod secretariat tried to muzzle the bishops themselves by telling them to hold no press conferences or make speeches unless the secretariat approved. Many bishops held meetings with the press anyway. Poland's conservative Stefan Cardinal Wyszynski attacked the press on the synod floor for distorting church affairs by "politicizing" its accounts. He appealed for strict secrecy, criticized his talkative colleagues, and said comments on the floor should never be divulged without the permission of the speaker. In contrast, the Vatican press office, under its new director Heston, made it the first truly open synod. The briefings were so complete that one U. S. newsman was heard to grumble that he wished he could get a refund on the $35 he had paid to attend daily inside-dope press conferences by an independent organization.

Three special institutions have reinforced the Catholic secrecy culture: the code of canon law, the Vatican Archives, and the Holy office.

The Code of Canon Law—The church is investing many years in a comprehensive reform of the existing law code of 1917. In 1968 the Canon Law Society of America held a symposium on the need for a church "bill of rights" in the new code. In a position paper from that meeting, this distinguished group affirmed the following as an inalienable right:

> The right of individuals to access to objective information, in particular about the internal and external operations of the Church. We believe that man is free only when he understands himself, his society, and his place within it. We believe there should be no arbitrary restrictions placed upon man's ability to acquire information necessary to this understanding. In this respect, the freedom of the press is an essential Christian freedom.

In the international scholarly journal *Concilium* the following year, a group of canonists similarly proposed a right to information in a church bill of rights modeled after the United Nations Universal Declaration of Human Rights. The Concilium secretariat commented that "at least at the level of central government, the usual ecclesiastical policy of presuming the necessity of secrecy and of only occasionally allowing publicity should be reversed, so that the necessity of publicity is presumed and secrecy only occasionally imposed when there are compelling reasons for it." Despite such efforts the secret provisional drafts for the new code which were leaked to the press did not mention the right to information. Meanwhile, the U.S. canonists have complained that the secrecy in drafting of revisions is hindering their contributions to the new code.

The present code of canon law is one of the bulwarks against the opening up of the church. Secrecy is referred to in fifteen of the canons. Most of them deal with protection of pastoral information and of the reputation of accused persons in church courts. However, secrecy extends to all elections, from the papacy on down, and any interference by the laity invalidates a vote. Staff members of the

Roman Curia are bound by an oath of total secrecy, and this example is widely followed throughout the church. At the April 1969 consistory where 33 men were made cardinals, a new oath was added to the ceremony after the traditional vow of loyalty to Christ and the pope:

> I will not divulge to their damage or discredit the *consilia* [deliberations] entrusted to me, either directly or indirectly, without the consent of the Holy See.

The canons require many reports, but they all go *up*, from administrator to bishop, from bishop to the Vatican, or from officials of an order to the Vatican. Other canons require locked diocesan archives for official records which cannot be entered without the bishop's personal permission. Elaborate protective measures are involved, including the use of double locks with the keys held by two different men. Nonsecret archives are supposed to be available to a person with a "legitimate interest," if the diocesan chancellor approves. The most important fact about the present code of canon law is that it does not *require* disclosure of any kind of information to the people.

The Vatican Archives—The repository of historical documents has also perpetuated a tradition of secrecy in the church. The strict closed-door policy in the past meant that the translators of the King James Version, the standard English Protestant Bible for centuries, never had access to the "Codex Vaticanus," one of the major Bible manuscripts from the fourth century. The Council of Trent had made Jerome's Latin translation the basis for Catholic Bibles, which left the Greek text of little interest. Bible scholars never got to study the Codex until Napoleon stole the archives and took them to Paris as a prize of war.

The rules today, described by Maria Luisa Ambrosini in *The Secret Archives of the Vatican* (1969), are more liberal. The rooms which contain highly classified documents dealing with living persons and still-existing situations are locked, as would be the case with many secular governments. All of the documents are off limits to newsmen, but since 1881 the nonsensitive papers have been available to scholars who pass scrutiny. Direct application must be made to the pope on a "need to know" basis. After screening, about 200 persons per year are admitted to the archives.

The Vatican maintains a "100 years" rule, making material from most of the last century unavailable. In 1969 Pope Paul authorized publication of all the documents from Vatican Council I (1869–1870). The Vatican is more open than the government of Italy, which refused to open the royal archives to a reputable British historian preparing a standard work on the 1840–1870 era. The principals had been dead for nearly a century. The French and British use a 30-year rule. The United States traditionally requires a 20-year wait, but long after 1965, scholars have been unable to see mountains of material from World War II. In 1972 President Nixon ordered that after 10 years, secret national security and diplomatic material could be reviewed for declassification. But the documents must be specified so that they can be obtained with "a reasonable amount of effort," which is difficult because only the insiders know what is in the files. The person or newspaper making the request is supposed to pay the considerable cost of the search, even if the security screeners decide that the material cannot be declassified. A mass of material at the Vatican remains "secret" in the sense that it has never even been inventoried. The officials do not know what is there and what is not.

An interesting question on historical documents is whether they belong to the institution or to the individual. For example, the late Eugene Cardinal Tisserant, archivist and adviser to five popes, is reported to have kept detailed diaries which contained excerpts of many Vatican documents over the decades. When he died in 1973, church officials hauled a dozen suitcases of documents from his home. The cardinal's niece-housekeeper-secretary, Paule Hennequin, hired a lawyer and contended that as sole heir and executor she was entitled to all personal papers that were not church property. There were also widespread rumors that the conservative cardinal had shipped some of his papers to France or Switzerland shortly before his death. In the midst of the dispute *Paris Match* published an article, supposedly based on the Tisserant papers, claiming that Pope Pius XI had been poisoned by a Vatican doctor on orders of Mussolini, whose mistress was the doctor's daughter. The Vatican denied the report, although observers theorized that Tisserant might have written it down as gossip, rather than as established fact.

The Holy Office—Until its recent name change to the Congregation for the Doctrine of the Faith and various reforms in procedure, the Vatican's theological watchdog agency was one of the most-discussed enforcers of secrecy. In the old days anyone could denounce a scholar's work to the office and know that his identity would be kept secret. Thus the defendant had no right to confront his accusers. The criteria on which it judged works were never released, the writer typically had no idea his book was under attack, and had no opportunity to defend himself. English historian H. P. R. Finberg wrote in 1964, "Not without reason has the Holy Office been described as the most arbitrary tribunal in the civilized world."

Many contemporary theologians have suffered under the old office's secrecy system. What was apparently the last of the agency's old-fashioned secret Star Chamber trials was conducted in June 1968 on Monsignor Ivan Illich, the director of the controversial Center for Intercultural Documentation in Cuernavaca, Mexico. Called to Rome to answer charges, Illich passed through double doors, corridors, staircases, and an elevator into a basement inner sanctum. There a judge who declined to give his name began the interrogation. But Illich refused to play the game under the traditional rules, and stalled things at the start by refusing to take the initial oath of secrecy. He argued that this procedure violated a new ruling from Pope Paul that the office's procedures be a matter of public record. He also refused to answer questions until a list of charges had been presented. He was later given a set of 85 are-you-still-beating-your-wife type questions, many drawn from anonymous accusations. Sample: "How do you

respond to those who present you as 'petulant, adventurous, impru-
dent, fanatical and hypnotizing, a rebel to any authority' . . .?" Illich
refused to respond to such a dehumanizing questionnaire. Half a year
after this inconclusive investigation his center was declared off limits
to the world's priests. Shortly thereafter, Illich left the priesthood.

In most areas of Vatican life significant improvements have been
made in recent years, and yet for every step forward there seems to
be a half-step back. However, the general pattern is in the direction
of openness toward the public. The current ambivalence is part of a
venerable institution in transition. If changes are to be made, one of
the major influences will be the example of the church in the United
States, which is second only to Italy and Brazil among the nations in
on-paper membership, and is the most important Catholic country in
terms of active members and money.

3 Secrecy—American Style

Sometimes history is made in almost humdrum fashion. There was no particular tingle of excitement at 9:30 A.M. on April 11, 1972, as 75 of us reporters filed past uniformed door guards into a large meeting room at Atlanta's Sheraton-Biltmore. The meeting we were covering turned out to be relentlessly routine. Despite that, the event was extraordinary. The bishops of the Catholic church in the United States were opening their deliberations to the church and secular press, and to 23 invited observers from the clergy, religious orders, and laity. This had never before been permitted in the U.S., or hardly anywhere else, in modern times. The U.S. bishops' move to an open-door policy was the end of an era in which secrecy was virtually an unquestioned fact in policy formulation. The next stage, likely to be lengthy and filled with advances and retreats, will be the application of openness in Catholic life at all levels, down to the parish and up to the Vatican.

The start toward U.S. openness was not achieved easily or automatically, and neither will be the future extensions. Monsignor Vincent Yzermans laments that "the right to information is scandalously ignored in many areas of church administration." Yzermans' assistant and short-term successor, layman Gerald Renner, is even more blunt:

Secrecy has been elevated to such an art that the observer sometimes thinks of it as one of the hallmarks of the One True Church. I'm afraid that a mystique of secrecy will continue to prevail throughout the administrative structures of the Church until such time as those structures are changed to admit to some form of accountability to the faithful. So far, the information process has been restricted on a *"need* to know" basis, not unlike our government intelligence services. This despite the fact that there is a preponderance of theological weight behind a *"right* to know." It's just that few in any position of authority within the Church pay any attention to it. Some progressive parishes that have lay boards of real authority have begun to cut through the veil of secrecy, because the only way intelligent decisions can be made is through informed opinion. But so long as decision-making at the diocesan, national, and world levels of the Church is confined to a clerical few, there is no real urgency to admit to a "right to know."

Such conditions in the secular government would, no doubt, produce an indignant howl from the Catholic citizenry.

When the bishops of the United States first set up their Bureau of Information (now the National Catholic Office for Information) in 1937 to deal with the secular media, it was not so much to provide information as to act as a "defender of the faith," responding to accusations or misinterpretations. The bishops had tight control over most of the Catholic press, in which they had made a major investment, and by contrast with these "house organs" the secular press was meddlesome. Besides that, many figured, why should the secular press get information for free when the Catholic papers had to pay for it through the National Catholic News Service? At a seminar run by the information office years ago a daily newspaper editor groused about this attitude:

On a Monday the wires carry a few lines of a significant story about which our readers would like to know more. I try in vain for 30 minutes to get a Catholic source to comment. No comment. I phone the Catholic editor on Monday, Tuesday, and Wednesday. He says he has no information. Then I read my copy of the Catholic paper on Thursday night and suddenly he has *plenty* of information. The Monday story isn't "news" by Friday, so we pass it up. Then next week he runs an editorial stating that "only in the Catholic paper last week was story X" and that the local daily ignores significant Catholic stories. At the same time he holds back a good story from me, he blasts me for not running it!

Under Monsignor John E. Kelly (1955–1962) the national office encouraged the increase of information bureaus in local dioceses from 35 to 86, out of the 156 dioceses. However, many of the directors were priests who edited the local Catholic papers, and thus had a proprietary interest in keeping news to themselves. Kelly also tried to emphasize the "information" rationale for his office. In one booklet he hoped out loud that "U.S. Catholic newsmakers may come to see the potential of the mass media, with even a modicum of cooperation from the church, to get significant and accurate Catholic information to the non-Catholic public—with incalculable gains of good will for the church."

Renner, who later became the Maryland director of the National Conference of Christians and Jews, aided Kelly for three years, and then returned to work with Monsignor Yzermans. He succeeded Yzermans in 1967 as director, but soon left in a dispute, making public complaints about the headquarters attitude that "the actions of the bishops are no one else's business."

Renner recalls that in the Kelly days the national office handled mostly routine matters. The bishops would assemble in Washington, D.C., each November under conditions roughly as open as a meeting of the Politburo. At the end of the meeting the information bureau would be handed the bishops' pastoral statement, reaffirming various traditional views. It was mailed to all newspapers, with a Sunday embargo so the weekly Catholic papers would not be scooped. The bureau then compiled the news play and editorial reaction to the statement and sent a report on this to the bishops which, for some inexplicable reason, was "confidential."

The hottest stories in the old days were the announcements of the appointments of new bishops by the Vatican. The security system the church used for these announcements in Washington was reminiscent of that followed across the river at the Pentagon. The word would come on Tuesday afternoons from the Apostolic Delegate's residence. An envelope bearing the bold legend "By Safe Hand Only" would be taken across town to the offices of the National Catholic Welfare Conference (now called the U.S. Catholic Conference) by the Delegate's taciturn chauffeur, or an equally sober-faced monsignor. A news release would be written in Kelly's office, then run off in a mimeographing room behind a locked, guarded door. Late Tuesday the release would be hand-carried to Associated Press and United Press International, marked for release at 8:00 A.M. Wednesday, the day the appointments were announced in *L'Osservatore Romano*. When officials learned of the advance releases to the wire services, they clamped down, and Kelly's messenger was not to cross the threshold of the news bureaus until 8:00 A.M. Wednesday. But the secrecy system did not work so efficiently in Rome, and there is also a time difference. So the U.S. bishops' messenger often ended up handing the Washington news bureaus a "flash" that had come in from Rome hours before. Kelly never got a hint a new appointment was coming until the Safe Hand arrived, and at least once he got caught flatfooted. One week the office kept getting inquiries about the appointment of a new auxiliary to Francis Cardinal Spellman in New York. It turned out that the anxious appointee had mixed up his Wednesdays and mentioned his new status at morning Mass a week too soon.

Another task of the information bureau, as Renner describes it, was to serve as a buffer between the press and the Apostolic Delegate. Since the Delegate's office had an unlisted phone number, journalists had to work through the information bureau to ask for an interview. In his 25 years in the post Archbishop (later Cardinal) Amleto Cicognani routinely rejected the requests. His successor, Archbishop (now Cardinal) Egidio Vagnozzi, readily agreed to talk but turned out to be, in Renner's terms, "a sort of ecclesiastical Spiro Agnew." In a chat with the White House women's press corps he embarrassed the Americans by describing his job as Delegate as "keeping an eye" on the bishops to make sure they were orthodox.

The U.S. visit of Julius Cardinal Döpfner in 1966 provided a test case of the power plays the American hierarchy sometimes used to suppress unsettling ideas, even from a fellow bishop. Döpfner was the vice chairman of the commission then advising the pope on what to say about birth control. That year a secret directive to priests in his diocese, apparently with Döpfner's approval, said couples who decided they had good reason to practice artificial contraception should not be refused the sacraments. The story was widely reported, although due to official pressure it was never mentioned in the National Catholic News Service. Then when Döpfner was to visit the U.S., an American archbishop interceded to kill plans to have the cardinal speak at one of the well-publicized luncheons at the National Press Club. The cardinal had his press conference anyway, sponsored by the German Embassy at a downtown hotel in Washington. He diplomatically sidestepped comment on birth control, because the question was under study by the pope.

In November 1966 the American bishops were to gather at Catholic University for their first meeting since the close of Vatican II. This was a watershed meeting for the bishops' information policy. Even at this late date there was surprisingly strong pressure to shut the windows that had been opened in Rome to accommodate the press. Two weeks before the meeting the information office was informed that there would be only three press conferences during the five-day meeting. Worse yet, admittance would be limited to news services such as the A.P., U.P.I., and N.C. News. This would keep out such troublemakers as John Cogley of the *New York Times* and the writers for independent Catholic papers. The information staff hoped to change this when the bishops' administrative board met the Saturday before the meeting opened, but the press relations problem was not even on the agenda. Several bishops on the board managed to force the issue, and the bishops decided to permit daily, open press briefings for the first time. With no budget, Yzermans and his crew scrounged around town overnight in search of typewriters to put together a decent press room.   **1795725**

With these daily briefings a crack appeared in the door to the meetings. Reporters could get enough leads to piece together what was happening inside. This proved upsetting to traditionalists, who remembered the days when the bishops spoke with an artificially united voice through prepared statements, and could come to their conferences without public notice. When candid reports of the closed-door discussions began surfacing in the newspapers, the bishops hired uniformed private detectives to guard the doors of their meetings. The information office began holding press panels with bishops, a la Vatican II, but the comments were often cautious. Renner theorizes, "Bishops are probably more afraid of other bishops than their priests are of them."

At the time the bishops' spokesman at the press briefings was Minnesota's Auxiliary Bishop James Shannon. He would take longhand notes in the meetings, clear them with an officer of the bishops' conference, and twice a day meet the press. Shannon recalls putting a shocking idea before the bishops at the November 1968 meeting, the last one before he submitted his resignation from the episcopate:

> I very hesitatingly and gingerly suggested that the bishops open their meetings to the press. Executive sessions could be voted if certain topics were very sensitive, but we were making *everything* an executive session. When there was this much secrecy, it gave the public the impression that we had more to hide than to show. The bishops were shortchanging themselves on a lot of progressive steps they were taking. In the discussion, various bishops talked of reporters in terms of voyeurism and keyhole-peeping. Finally, one cardinal said to me, "Young man, would you tell this body one advantage that would come from opening these meetings?" And I replied, "It would vastly improve the quality of the debate."

One result of the bishops' closed-door attitude was that some editors began questioning whether it was worthwhile sending a reporter to cover the meetings. And once having enjoyed press exposure, the bishops wanted to continue it. Another result was the start of press keyhole-peeping. In November 1970 two reporters managed the logistically difficult feat of listening in on the sessions at the Washington Hilton. After the April 1971 meeting in Detroit, Hiley Ward of the *Detroit Free Press* wrote about his snooping exploits in the *News Letter* of the Religion Newswriters Association, the secular press group of which he was then president. Ward's original plot was to dress like a maintenance man, carry a *Free Press* ladder into the meeting room before the session, use it to climb to the balcony, then pull up the ladder after him. The first day all that effort proved unnecessary. He simply walked into the balcony and watched from behind a pole until he was caught by the guards. Then Ward and former Jesuit seminarian James Bowman of the *Chicago Daily News* figured out a way to lie on the floor behind a curtain on the ballroom platform, cramped between a piano and stacks of chairs. Ward boasted, "I suspect it would take 50 policemen, a budget of $50,000, and some know-how from the F.B.I. to really keep us out. Alternatives would be to have the bishops meet in an open field, ringed by National Guardsmen touching elbows, or else high up in a cloud out of sight." Some secular reporters, however grateful for the tips they picked up from the journalistic gumshoes, had doubts about these tactics.

After Shannon resigned, his modest proposal to open the meetings was taken up by the bishops' communications staff, notably two shrewd laymen, Robert Beusse and Russell Shaw. The communications committee which advises the bishops proposed to their April 1970 meeting that some sessions be opened on a trial basis. The proposal mentioned only the sessions when they met as the U.S. Catholic Conference, which deals with national program and social issues on which the bishops desired to get more publicity. It did not include the contiguous meetings of the bishops as the National Conference of Catholic Bishops, which handles ecclesiastical matters. Most of the recent controversy, and press interest, has come in the

N.C.C.B. sessions. While the U.S.C.C. is a long-standing civil corporation which cuts across diocesan lines, the N.C.C.B. is a new entity in the church line of authority, which traditionally has run from the Vatican directly to the individual bishop and diocese.

The committee built its case for open meetings on the practical benefits. For instance, the openness would end distortions of the meetings created by reporting via leaks, enhance the bishops' "credibility," and head off the publicity gained by outside lobbying groups and hangers-on. (At the first open meeting, in Atlanta, a lone Tennessee priest stood out on the street in a light rain holding a hand-lettered announcement of his grievances. In the days of secret meetings reporters with time on their hands might have smothered the father with coverage.) The committee's argument was from prudence, rather than from theology and ethics. At the bishops' meeting the proposal proved surprisingly popular. Only a preliminary decision to require a two-thirds margin for approval killed the idea, by a 130-to-67 eyelash. Archbishop Philip Hannan of New Orleans, unwilling to let the idea die at that point, quickly put through a motion that set up a study committee.

The following July this reporter represented the Religion Newswriters Association at a hearing with the new committee, which was led by Archbishop Francis Furey of San Antonio. Most of the time was spent on procedures for screening reporters, to help sell the idea to bishops who feared opening up also to observers from Catholic interest groups. The Religion Newswriters Association's position was that all U.S.C.C. and N.C.C.B. sessions should be open, but the bishops' committee ruled out discussion of the N.C.C.B. In a later report to the religion reporters I said, "The bishops are anxious to get publicity on what they are doing in the action areas covered by U.S.C.C., and they dislike coverage of hallway agitators. While this may be a tribute to the alleged 'power of the press,' it means the bishops have not really faced the question of their *responsibility* to their N.C.C.B. constituency (which, after all, includes our readers)."

The Furey report of November 1970 improved on the communications committee's proposal in two ways. First, it asked that *all* U.S.C.C. meetings be open, except for executive sessions. Second, it added an excellent rationale from Catholic theology to the pragmatic arguments in the earlier proposal. Despite the impressive case made, the Furey committee report went down to a crushing defeat (51 yes, 148 no). The rumors from inside the meeting attributed the flip-flop from the bishops' vote earlier in the year to ire over a *New York Times* page one story on the opening day of the meeting. It dealt with charges of church financial secrecy. The secret debate on secrecy was salted with antipress remarks, led by four of the U.S. cardinals at the meeting:

James Francis Cardinal McIntyre of Los Angeles, the 84-year-old dean of the hierarchy, objected that "some reporters have no background in theology, and we're dealing with souls and consciences." (The same argument, of course, would exclude most Catholics from being able to comprehend the discussions as well. But many religion reporters these days *do* have academic training in the field.)

Patrick Cardinal O'Boyle of Washington, D.C., still smarting from the publicity over a priestly rebellion over birth control, said he, for one, did not expect a "fair hearing" from reporters. And "there are some things we want among ourselves," such as planning tactics for influencing the government.

Conservative John Cardinal Carberry of St. Louis feared that if the meetings were opened to the press, this would lead to opening them up to representatives of priests' groups and other Catholic organizations. He said that Vatican II had recognized the right to information but neither the Council nor the subsequent Synods of Bishops were open.

John Cardinal Cody of Chicago complained, "The press no longer reports the news; they make it." And, he cautioned, "a decision once made can't be retracted."

Bishop Gerald McDevitt, auxiliary to Philadelphia's John Cardinal

Krol, said that if the press came in, "there would be more distortion than there is now, not less. The press ignores the substantial things now," such as the hierarchy's statements against abortion.

Bishop Christopher Weldon of Springfield, Massachusetts, was afraid that if reporters were admitted his colleagues might "talk more to the press than to the bishops."

And Bishop Hugh Donohoe of Fresno, California, remarked, "The press is wonderful—in its place. But this isn't the place."

A good summary of the conservative mindset was provided after the meeting in a column by Catholic journalist Dale Francis. He said the bishops need the freedom "to say what they think, and express opposition to the positions of other bishops, without this dialogue being reported in the press." Some bishops might feel intimidated, while others might become headline-seekers. Also, he said, the disruption of some Protestant meetings by demonstrators showed that churchmen must be able to "discuss their problems without outside influence." This lack of confidence in the leadership of the church was striking. The bishops were supposedly so immature that if faced with public exposure they would either be afraid to say what they thought, or become publicity-seekers.

Part of the bishops' distrust of the secular press was the usual reaction of officials when troublesome stories are printed. On the other hand, various bishops had legitimate complaints about certain past stories. Journalists are far from infallible. But in the case of Catholicism the remarkable thing is that coverage has not been *more* distorted. Many of the important archbishops have been virtually incommunicado from the press for years. A survey by the U.S.C.C. Communications Department found that only 14 per cent of the bishops responding had given any interviews to the secular press in the first three months of 1973. Other results: 55 per cent did not have a practice of occasional off-the-record discussions with media people, and 46 per cent did not have a communications advisory group that included media representatives. In an all-too-typical action the Philadelphia Archdiocese stopped sending press announcements to the jointly owned *Inquirer* and the *News* in 1973, thus giving the edge to the competing *Bulletin.* The chancery said the two papers had not "come to grips with certain issues," but speculation was that it was a reprisal for a *News* story that identified a girl getting an abortion as a Catholic.

The daily press has been under considerable pressure in covering the bishops' meetings, and till fairly recently it got little help in the task. A major breakthrough came when the bishops decided to release the basic documents and reports prepared in advance of the meetings. With statements that were formulated during the meetings, however, reporters operated under severe difficulty in the days of secret meetings. A memorable case was in November 1968 when the U.S. bishops had to decide what to say in the wake of Pope Paul's encyclical reaffirming the church ban on artificial birth control. It was a major story, because of the widespread dissent from the encyclical by American priests. After a week of leaks and rumors about the bishops' discussions, the final statement was released at noon on Friday. As reporters for the afternoon papers and the wire services grasped madly for the limited available copies, Bishop (now Cardinal) John J. Wright led a press panel through a meandering theological explanation of the complex statement. The key issue was whether the bishops were backing the pope to the hilt, or whether they were allowing room for some honest disagreement. The document itself was deliberately ambiguous and the press briefing did nothing to clarify matters, so various news accounts stressed certain passages in an attempt to decipher the bishops' intent. Then some bishops, quoting other sections, accused the press of distortion.

The final push in favor of opening the meetings came from Rome, albeit under the influence of various Americans. Half a year after the bishops strongly rejected open meetings, the Pontifical Commission on the Means of Social Communication issued its "Pastoral Instruction" as a sequel to the Vatican II decree on the media. The document,

approved by Pope Paul, asserted the necessity of openness and freedom of information within the church. Although the commission did
not specifically address the issue of open meetings, the results came
quickly.

The bishops decided to set up yet another committee to study the
question. This panel, led by Bishop Raymond Gallagher of Lafayette,
Indiana, proposed that not only reporters but representatives of the
diocesan clergy, religious orders, and laity be admitted to meetings of
both the U.S.C.C. and the N.C.C.B., subject to a call for an executive
session. The debate at the bishops' meeting in November 1971 was
magically transformed from that of a year earlier, due largely to the
Pastoral Instruction. While the opponents, led by Cardinal Carberry,
repeated the objections from the previous year, other bishops appealed
for the hierarchy to take the long view and forgive journalistic sins
of the past. Detroit's Cardinal Dearden, concluding his term as president of the bishops' conference, reportedly let it be known that he
favored the change. Eventually the bishops voted in favor of admitting
the press, 144 to 106 (now only a simple majority was needed for
passage). Then the bishops discussed separately the matter of admitting nonparticipating observers from the church at large. In a speech
which was not mentioned in the press briefing after the debate, Cardinal McIntyre warned: "My dear boys, we are on dangerous ground.
Are we a hierarchy, or a democratic organization? This is in direct
or indirect opposition to the Holy Father. If we go ahead, we are
inviting the crashing of our own heads" (i.e., suicide). But the second
motion passed even more handily: 169 to 76.

In the same period the Conference of Major Superiors of Men,
consisting of the leaders of U.S. men's orders, had opened its annual
assemblies and business meetings both to the press and to any other
observers who wished to attend. The Canadian bishops met prior to
the 1971 world Synod of Bishops and invited reporters into half of the
sessions, but the policy has been in flux. In April 1972 about one-third
of the meetings were open. But in October 1972 all the sessions were

secret. The Canadian Catholic Conference issued a statement explaining that "normally" all "plenary sessions" of the bishops would be in secret. It said that the earlier open meetings were "information sessions, workshops, and committee of the whole" and that some of these would continue to be open. Unlike the U.S. bishops, the Canadians made no provision for regular observers from the clergy, religious, and laity. In the U.S. a continuing issue is whether the spring meetings of the hierarchy in 12 regional groupings will be open like the fall meetings of the entire hierarchy. A group of Catholic editors has issued a statement praising those bishops who opened their regional discussions. As for the secrecy holdouts, "we deplore with vigor the attitude of some that the people of God do not have a right to know or—worse—that they are not interested in what the bishops are discussing."

The U.S. bishops faced a delicate "right to know" issue when they ordered a $500,000 research project on the priesthood. Inevitably, the resulting reports got into a series of nettlesome issues. The bishops were particularly critical of the theological report authored by Carl Armbruster, a Jesuit who has since left the priesthood. The document concluded that there was no theological basis for barring women from the priesthood, that celibacy was a distinct gift that should not be required of all priests, and that the traditional view of apostolic succession was in error. Long after the contents of the report had been leaked to the *New York Times,* the leaders of the bishops' conference said it would be "misleading" to publish it officially because the bishops do not agree with the conclusions. This problem of seeming "endorsement" of the revisionist ideas apparently was the major factor in the decision not to publish the report, rather than simple censorship of unpleasant material. The hierarchy did decide to distribute the companion reports on history, psychology, and sociology, which included equally embarrassing findings.

What did reporters think about the open meetings that they had pressed for? Previously they had been able to piece together a reasonably accurate account of what went on, but now they were able to size up the bishops as men, watch them interact, understand fully the context in which statements are made, and observe the full range of discussion, instead of depending on secondhand briefings and news releases after the fact. Direct quotes were possible at last. There were some mixed feelings, however. Instead of kibitzing over coffee in the press room or floating around town looking for other story ideas, reporters found themselves sitting through hours of canned reports and housekeeping items. The major gain had been made, not by the press, but by the Catholic church. The bishops discovered that in this area, at least, they could be authentically Catholic and open in style, seem less aloof from their constituency, gain "credibility," and exhibit their own growing self-confidence as a body.

Conservate editor Francis, who had attacked the open-meetings proposal, remarked with a smile, "I'll have to say that I was wrong." Another man known to oppose open meetings was John Cardinal Krol, a traditionalist who became president of the bishops' conference just in time to preside over the first open meeting. He said he was "very pleased" with the way things went. In his presidential address at Atlanta Krol made a droll reference to the past press escapades: "The openness of this meeting will eliminate the aura of mystery, and it may eliminate the discomforts endured by the more adventurous who in the past, through their ingenuity, tried to penetrate the mystery." Afterward, Krol spotted erstwhile eavesdropper Hiley Ward in the hallway and said, "I gave you a free commercial and you didn't even say thank you."

4 God's Mammon

Back when the U.S. bishops met in secret, Bishop Shannon arrived in the press room one day for his regular noon briefing with reporters, only to announce that he had nothing to announce. Then with a bit of Irish wit he offered to fill up the rest of the press conference time by doing card tricks if anyone had a deck. What was so supersensitive that the bishops had taken the unusual measure of ordering Shannon to reveal absolutely nothing? Birth control? Priests getting married? It turned out that the topic of the morning had been a report suggesting that the dioceses issue regular financial reports.

One of the startling things about the *Official Catholic Directory* and the *Catholic Almanac* which come out yearly is that they contain no financial information. Most Protestant yearbooks in North America include a mind-numbing accounting of the fiscal facts of life. Many denominations publish a complicated breakdown on the budget of each congregation as part of the annual minutes. In the Catholic church in the U.S. and Canada, as elsewhere, it is anybody's guess how much money is coming in, how much is salted away in assets, and where the money is going. One of the many symbols of the old ethos is the strikingly modern St. Mary's Cathedral in San Francisco. The building project began in 1962 after the old cathedral burned down, and culminated in the dedication ceremony of May 1971. Throughout that decade Catholics in the archdiocese never knew how

much the project cost. Nor did they know at the time of the dedication, which was picketed by liberal groups protesting the heavy investment in a building instead of in meeting social needs.

Modern St. Mary's also symbolizes the changes in financial accountability, however, because the facts eventually were revealed
when the chancery office issued its first financial report in history. The
cathedral building, including furnishings, cost $10.9 million. The en-
tire complex, including a high school, demolition, and fund-raising
expenses, ran close to $16 million, more than many of the critics had
supposed. The fund-raising campaign, which included a few smaller
projects, ended up adding $1.5 million to the archdiocese's consider-
able debt. As a local priest remarked, "It took them ten years to tell
the people where things stood. The questions began in 1962, the
answers came in 1972."

Until the late 1960s any sort of diocesan financial report would have
been unthinkable. But then money started to become perhaps the
most intense secrecy issue in American Catholicism. Many dioceses
and parishes, usually under pressure, began issuing financial reports
of widely varying quality. And journalists went to work on the riddle
of finances in religious orders and the Vatican. The dim outlines of
Catholic wealth have started to emerge. Sensational reports have been
answered by denials and disclaimers from Catholic spokesmen, typically with an intriguing lack of details. And when the dust has settled
in a dispute about Catholic wealth, the case can usually be summarized in two words: Who knows?

Why the cover-up? Not, apparently, to hide corruption, although
if all the facts were known some officials might be exposed as inept.
Perhaps Catholics have held the naïve view that such matters interfere
with the "spiritual" quality of the church and should not be discussed
openly. The amazing lack of financial curiosity among the laity whose
offerings kept the church running was part of the waning Father-
knows-best era. Like the laity, the local fathers today no longer assume that Chancery-knows-best.

In many states the general public has been as curious as the Catholic laity about church finances, and rightly so. The church benefits from tax exemption and other economic privileges. Parochial schools participate in a wide range of public aid programs, and the church has been trying to expand this aid. Thus all taxpayers have a direct stake in financial information. The National Association of Laity, a liberal Catholic organization whose membership has dropped from a high of 13,000 to 4,000, has used these aid requests as a lever for opening the church books. In letters to Congressmen, Supreme Court briefs, and testimony before state legislatures, the lay group has taken on the officials of the church by arguing that full disclosure must precede public grants. As N.A.L. legal counsel Leo Jordan asked the Illinois legislature in 1971:

> How can you who have sworn to protect the interests of the citizens of Illinois vote for a $40 million grant if you are not certain whether the individual dioceses or parishes have monies of their own? The bishop is the absolute ruler of his diocese. If he wanted to provide you with evidence of need for financial assistance, that information would be here before you now.

These practical pressures may well be as influential as the bishops' devotion to accountability in the first steps that have been taken toward financial openness. Staff members of the Chicago chancery said that one reason the archdiocese expedited its first financial report was complaints from state legislators that they would not vote for school aid unless the books were opened. The Minnesota Civil Liberties Union and other foes of parochial aid went to court, seeking an order that all church finances be made public. Earlier the St. Paul archdiocese had issued a financial report, after gripes from laymen.

An eminent Catholic attorney, Wisconsin's William E. Brown, complained in *Can Catholic Schools Survive?* (1970) that laymen are expected to foot the bill while the parish clergy generally keep money matters to themselves and bishops set educational policy unilaterally.

Laymen may sit on advisory boards "but they may not go near the water of policy making, administration, cost information, and financing methods." He believes the schools cannot survive under this system. Decisions and support must be broadly based in the Catholic community so that the laity will support the schools even if state legislatures do not come through with any cash. Why not provide uniform cost accounting, subject to independent audit? After all, "directors and officers of business corporations have been forced out of office, or have been required to pay damages, or have been penalized by government regulatory agencies" for holding back the information necessary for investors to make intelligent decisions.

With the first strides toward financial openness, some bishops may have gone through a little agony as the membership for the first time has had a chance to judge their performance and to discern the church's priorities. But the long-term result will be a financially stronger church, according to James Gollin, author of *Worldly Goods* (1971), the best attempt yet at exposing Catholic financial secrets. Gollin contended that Catholics are concerned enough about church problems, and informed enough about investments, to want to know what their church is doing with its money. In this situation a bishop with clear and open investment policies will be better off financially than a bishop committed to the old spirit of mystery. When they learn the truth, Catholics "will be more responsive to appeals for new funds and less mistrustful of the financial competence of the hierarchy. In their turn, the bishops will be placed under pressure to make every investment dollar count."

How well has the secretive church performed? After five years of research, Gollin (a non-Catholic freelance writer) concluded that the U.S. Catholic church was an ill-managed outfit with barely enough liquid capital to keep its programs going. Some persons with intimate knowledge of chancery operations have said privately that Gollin pictured such penury that he must have been taken down the garden path by some bishops. But his book is the first careful, methodical study, and it bulges with facts that church members ought to know and don't. Churchmen seeking to raise money glowed at Gollin's description of their threadbare finances, which is ironic since, according to Gollin, they have consciously perpetuated a myth of economic power through the use of secrecy. Like Brown, he contended that secrecy has eroded efforts to raise public support for parochial schools. He maintained that to qualify for local, state, or federal aid, every diocese ought to release complete, independently appraised balance sheets. "Only if the bishops voluntarily produce such a complete study; and if the study does make evident the inability of the church to continue its schools, should state and federal officials begin to plan legislation."

Gollin said that the "famine of information" *within* the church has also caused trouble. Bishops are often misled as to the financial facts, and have careened off into ill-advised building programs. Bishops learn little from other bishops. Dioceses and religious orders do not share data. Most starved for information are the laity, who Gollin said should know more than they do, and want to know more. Secrecy hinders the church in raising support from its members, and in sharing ideas which could lead to a more sensible financial policy.

He also insisted that canon law must be rewritten to make bishops accountable to their people. The bishop is often the equivalent of the trustee in civil law. A trust involves a donor, a trustee, and a beneficiary for whose benefit the trust is established. But the church escapes the rules in civil law. If a Catholic sets up a trust to support an institution, the bishop acts both as trustee and, as legal owner of all diocesan institutions, the beneficiary. The bishop is legally accountable only to himself and the Vatican, while those who are to benefit from the trusts—the people—are legally entitled to no accounting whatsoever. Most bishops take full advantage of this situation and leave their priests and laity "totally unenlightened about investments." Whether or not lay Catholics are *morally* entitled to know about diocesan investments, Western law holds that a trustee subject to outside scrutiny will in fact do a better job than one who is not.

Gollin was at pains to deflate the wild speculations about Catholic wealth that have flourished along with the secrecy policy. One of the most irresponsible of the sensationalists who nourished the popular image of secret, sinister financial power was a convert from Catholicism, the late Episcopal Bishop James A. Pike. He wrote in *Playboy,* among other things, that the Jesuits had a controlling interest in the Bank of America, the nation's largest, and earned at least $250 million a year from their investments. Jesuits sputtered, but they have never made a full accounting of their holdings. By Gollin's reckoning, all the 500 religious orders in the nation combined hold only $150 million in cash and securities. As for the dioceses, he figured that their securities and commercial properties are worth nearly $1 billion, which is not really that much for such a huge, far-flung organization. Journalist Nino Lo Bello's book about U.S. finances, which flies on the high side, also puts the American Jesuits' annual income at $250 million. He claims that all Catholic units in the U.S. and Canada combined have assets of more than $80 billion and an annual income of nearly $12.5 billion. A potential point of comparison with these estimates is the wealth of the Church of England, which is roughly comparable in size to U.S. Catholicism but more favored in economic history. The Anglicans' income and total assets (including historic buildings with burdensome upkeep) have not been reported, but a researcher put the investment holdings and deposit funds at more than $1¼ billion.

Besides official church wealth, there is some fascinating lore about quasi-official Catholic organizations. In fact, the most sensational Catholic money story to date has involved, not a religious order or a diocese, but a charity, Boys Town. The famous orphanage outside Omaha, Nebraska, was started by Father Edward J. Flanagan in 1917 with a borrowed $90. Through much of Flanagan's life it was a hand-to-mouth operation, and the Father used to tell the local St. Vincent de Paul societies that it was a mortal sin for them to keep any surplus funds if human beings were in need. But when Boys Town got famous through the movie in which Spencer Tracy played Flanagan, a virtuoso fund-raiser named Ted Miller joined the team. Through the work of Miller and his successors, Boys Town now has a worth of well over $200 million, including a securities portfolio valued (very conservatively) at $157 million. Although the interest on such a nest egg is ample to operate the Town, it still spends millions to send the traditional tearjerker fund appeals to 34 million people and raises nearly $18 million a year. This means Boys Town has about three times the endowment of Notre Dame university, raises more money than the Greater New York United Fund, and would rank 372nd in assets on the *Fortune* 500 if it were a business corporation. All this for 700 boys.

The facts on this Great Plains goldmine were dug out in 1972 by the enterprising weekly *Sun* newspapers of Omaha, owned by self-made millionaire Warren Buffett and edited by Paul Williams. And the Tax Reform Act of 1969 made it possible. The law requires tax-exempt organizations to file a Form 990 with the Internal Revenue Service, listing their income and assets, with the form open to public inspection. The law exempts churches and church agencies, and—until the filing for calendar 1972—any "subordinate organization" covered by a group exemption letter issued to a church body. The Roman Catholic church had been granted such a group exemption for every organization listed in the *Official Catholic Directory,* which includes Boys Town, described as a "protective institution" of the Archdiocese of Omaha. But for some reason Boys Town filed a Form 990 for calendar 1970 anyway. Archbishop Daniel E. Sheehan, president of the Boys Town board, said "every charitable and religious organization is jumping on us for having filed it."

The *Sun* papers had to wait for the I.R.S. form because Boys Town had always flatly refused money questions from newsmen or donors. After it got the information, the *Sun* went to interview Monsignor Nicholas Wegner, director of Boys Town, who was evasive about the extent of the investments and even said "we're so deep in debt all the time." When the reporter cited the I.R.S. form, Wegner said "that's

confidential information. . . . That shouldn't be given out at all."
When the reporter said it was a public document, he said "Yes, I
know, but it's still confidential." And he stated his concern several
times that public awareness of the facts would reduce people's contributions. For similar reasons, presumably, Boys Town literature says
the institution receives no state or federal funds, although the *Sun*
figures that in fact it gets $200,000 a year from various aid programs.
The paper found Boys Town employees reluctant to tell anything, and
even the assistant postmaster of the village forced it to go to Washington, D.C., to get the public record of postal receipts.

Supposedly, even Boys Town's fabulous wealth-per-lad is peanuts
compared with the finances of the Vatican, a topic which has excited
story after story of speculation. In 1968 Lo Bello published a book
exposé on Vatican wealth. In it he said that the Vatican is "the only
sovereign state that never publishes a budget. . . . The fact that the
Vatican has been able to maintain this secrecy in an age when business
and economics are of prime interest is indeed remarkable." He
claimed that the Vatican owned 40 to 50 per cent of the shares traded
on Italy's stock exchanges, and said "even a conservative estimate of
its portfolio" showed a worth in excess of $5.6 billion. The Vatican
fumed, but it was two years before *L'Osservatore Romano* accused Lo
Bello of "fantastic exaggeration." The Vatican's response contained
some revealing financial facts, but was vague about insurance, construction, holding companies, and investments outside Italy. One of
the most embarrassing investments was the Vatican stake in Washington, D.C.'s Watergate complex—not because of the later, unrelated
scandals known by its name, but because of Watergate's image of
extravagant living at a time when the church is talking increasingly
about the plight of the poor. After Watergate was built, the Vatican
sold most of its shares in the S.G.I. construction company of Rome,
which had financed the project. But Lo Bello writes that "the two
firms that sell, rent and administer for Watergate are accountable to
the Vatican."

Gollin's careful estimate, vastly smaller than Lo Bello's, is that the

Vatican financial gnomes parlayed reparations from Mussolini into investments worth something like $300 million in Italy and $200 million elsewhere. But since the Vatican's responses have left so many hard facts lacking, speculation continues and anybody can make any outlandish claims he wants about Vatican largesse. However rich in investments, the Vatican is apparently "cash poor." Reports filtering out during 1972 said that the Vatican had had to sell property just to meet its payroll, and that it lacked the money needed to hold some of the scheduled international meetings that have mushroomed since Vatican II.

One of those new advisory commissions got into the secrecy question itself. The Council of the Laity, in a 1972 report following a Vatican consultation, emphasized "the need for openness in the institutional affairs of the church, for instance in the matter of finance as an example where secretiveness at any level is an obstacle to the deep commitment of many to the apostolic work."

In religious orders widespread secrecy still prevails, but such pressures are having their effect in diocesan and parish affairs, at least in the United States. Whatever their flaws and omissions, public financial statements are a major first step toward accountability. The decision on whether to release information, and how much to release, is up to the local bishop and parish priest. Among the slowest to respond are some of the giant archdioceses such as Newark, Boston, Brooklyn (which reported for the first time in 1973), and N.C.C.B. President Krol's Philadelphia (which did not report, but provided data for a nonsectarian study on the parochial school crisis).

How good are the first-generation reports that have been issued? The Ralph Nader of the financial secrecy issue has been Joseph O'Donoghue, a priest who was suspended in Washington, D.C., after he opposed the pope's birth control encyclical. His 1972 staff report for the National Association of Laity found serious deficiencies in the accounting of the four of the superarchdioceses which had by then issued statements: Chicago, New York, Los Angeles, and Detroit.

Chicago—A 1970 report from the largest archdiocese in the U.S. showed assets of $85.5 million, including $29.5 million in investments, with yearly expenses of nearly $36 million—slightly less than income. As with many other diocesan reports, O'Donoghue complained that this reported only the finances of the central chancery office, not the entire archdiocese. The report itself acknowledged that it omitted the parishes, and agencies such as Catholic Charities. The N.A.L. also wanted to know about the status of elementary schools, since tax aid had been sought.

However, a subsequent report issued at the end of 1971 was one of the most complete issued by any diocese, and included parish finances as well as the chancery operations. It showed assets of $119 million, including securities with a market value of $83.5 million. Real estate was valued at $12 million, not counting parish property, which had a value of $683 million for insurance purposes but was not counted in the financial statement as such, on the argument that its value as an asset is questionable. The collections in the 456 parishes yielded $64.4 million, of which $3.2 million was assessed to support chancery operations. The parochial schools cost $61.5 million to operate, with only $27.4 million covered by tuition and other fees, and the rest by parish offerings and archdiocesan subsidies.

New York—The first report in 1968 did not provide a full accounting even though the archdiocese was pleading poverty when lay teachers demanded more pay. Under "Assets" and "Liabilities," the archdiocese offered meaningless figures about personnel and institutions, not dollar amounts, and it provided no data on its stock and property holdings.

New York's Terence Cardinal Cooke served as head of a committee of bishops to work out a uniform system of financial reporting, and early in 1972 the archdiocese, following those new procedures, issued a vastly improved report. It showed a net worth of $643 million, but of that amount $563 million was in "single purpose" land, buildings, and equipment. The other net assets consisted of $51 million in cash and other liquid assets, and an endowment of $29 million—far less than the N.A.L. and others had speculate 1. Revenues totaled $126 million, slightly less than expenditures. The New York report underscored the importance of including parish accounts, since it showed that the local parishes hold almost four-fifths of the net assets and spend three-fourths of the funds.

Among the omissions in the second New York report is the cemetery operation, which in the Chicago report was a major factor in assets and income. The report offered no breakdown on the value of specific sites such as St. Patrick's Cathedral, a block of midtown land which the *New York Times* estimated is worth a minimum of $20 million. In reporting its investments for the first time, New York, like Chicago, did not list the companies in which it held an interest. Unlike Chicago, New York did not specify how much of educational spending went to schools and how much to other forms of religious education.

Los Angeles—The archdiocese's 1970 statement reported only assets—no liabilities, no income, and no expenses. The N.A.L. said the assets list excluded some real property and investments.

Detroit—The archdiocese of John Cardinal Dearden was criticized for offering no data on parish and school finances in the year ending June 30, 1971, during which it shut down 63 schools. The cemetery account had invested as much as $20 million in the reported archdiocesan loan account, but the obviously well-heeled account itself was among the many special funds that were omitted. The report did not provide a capital value for its real estate holdings and equipment, on the argument that the figure would have been misleading.

The N.A.L. also stressed that many of the reports have not been audited. The auditors of the Peoria report said "we express no opinion on the accompanying balance sheet" because of the essential data that was not made available. (The diocesan newspaper did not report this disclaimer.) In the Baltimore archdiocese the accountants noted that they were told to exclude two fund-raising campaigns and high school data, both of which would be necessary to judge the financial situation. And on the Pittsburgh report the C.P.A. firm of Arthur Young & Co. noted: "Inasmuch as our engagement did not contemplate an examination in accordance with generally accepted auditing standards, we are unable to express an opinion on the accompanying financial statement."

Other oddities cited by the N.A.L.: Harrisburg, Pennsylvania, showed a near-doubling in investments from one year to the next. In Milwaukee half the funds raised for charity ended up being used for debt retirement. In Santa Fe the 1969 report said a number of real estate holdings had not been recorded, but there was no mention of this unrecorded property in the next year's report. Phoenix listed a transfer of $135,000 from the Diocese of Tucson, but the Tucson report made no mention of it. In Wichita half the $1 million proceeds from sale of a high school went to a separate fund not included in the report. Similarly, the St. Louis cemetery account contributed $156,000 to an unlisted account. In Davenport, Iowa, $250,000 in "restricted funds" was inexplicably changed into "disposable funds," and $396,000 worth of securities not listed in the previous year's report turned up for a contribution toward a new corporation.

Many of the reports covered only cash income and outgo, without a standard balance sheet. This avoids mention of the worth of investments. If a diocese puts its money in low-gain, high-yield securities, they would be nearly invisible on an income list. Most of the reports were not itemized in any detail. The N.A.L. charged that the practice almost everywhere of leaving out the finances of the nation's 18,000 parishes is "misleading and ethically questionable," unless the report states specifically that it is incomplete.

Just the opposite tack was taken by the Philadelphia archdiocesan advisory committee on the Catholic school crisis. A blizzard of financial statistics came with the report, obviously part of a well-laid strategy to get public funding. But the financial report on the archdiocese only added up the $60.7 million in receipts and $61.9 million in expenses of the parishes. Nothing was said about chancery finances, investments, auxiliary organizations, or other facets that would be needed to get a true picture of the Catholic plight.

The U.S. hierarchy's information director, Russell Shaw, issued a response to O'Donoghue's report which defended the bishops' record. He pointed out that four-fifths of the dioceses had made, or planned to make, public reports. The bishops' conference has set up seminars to train officials in the system based on Cardinal Cooke's committee recommendations for standard diocesan reporting. "The N.A.L. has chosen to ignore all this and indulge instead in negative carping about alleged shortcomings. This is a classic case of a self-appointed 'watch-dog' barking up the wrong tree."

The N.A.L. also charged that bishops around the nation spend $6 million a year of their supposedly limited funds to lobby for parochial school aid. A statement from the U.S. Catholic Conference retorted that the figure was "wildly inflated." But, typically, it provided no enlightenment on what the bishops actually do spend on lobbying. Once again, the conclusion was: Who knows? On money, as on most things, the church has had an ambivalent policy on information. It has made the initial commitment to seek an open style, and it has taken dramatic new steps, e.g., the diocesan financial reports. But secrecy persists.

Part II

THE SECRECY
TRADITION

5   *Disciplina Arcani*

What were the origins of the tradition of secrecy in the Catholic church? How did the practice develop, and why? The history of secrecy (appropriately enough) is rather inaccessible, since the minutiae of church administration are not always recorded for the ages. However, the story can be pieced together. In Catholicism the secrecy tradition is partly the result of good, or at least understandable, motives. Study of the history shows that the secrecy tradition has been variable, and that secrecy practices are not a necessary feature of Catholicism. Many of the harshest instances of it are a relatively late development, resulting from the peculiar hostilities of the nineteenth century, and have often been carried over without examination to the current, vastly changed situation.

All religions have a secretive aspect, of course, but not in the sense of withholding information. They have an awareness of mystery, a sense of reserve accorded to sacred precincts. Or they practice occasional withdrawal from those who do not believe. Secrecy in this more general sense has been an element in the Christian church from its beginnings. On the other hand, the openness and candor of the Bible is striking when it is compared with other ancient religious and secular annals. Instead of sanitized saints and do-no-wrong kings, the Bible describes a manic King Saul and a schemingly adulterous King David; battles lost as well as battles won; a doubting Thomas and a denying Peter. The Bible also honors communication, because it tells of a God who is intelligent and self-revealing, and who was incarnate in the person of Jesus.

Jesus advocated a sense of reserve and good taste in the religious life. He condemned public display of fasting, praying, and charity. Besides that, there is the question of the "secrecy sayings" of Jesus, which have been much-discussed in modern New Testament scholarship. These sayings apply to the sacred mysteries, not to the equivalent of information about church affairs. Jesus commanded secrecy about his person or his activities in three sayings to demons, two to disciples, four connected with miracles, and after St. Peter's confession and the Transfiguration. Mark is the "secrecy" gospel, since with one exception Matthew and Luke record the secrecy commands only in passages which parallel Mark and they sometimes omit Mark's secrecy material.

Many scholars would say that the secrecy sayings are not historical. In 1901 Germany's Wilhelm Wrede proposed his "messianic secret" theory. He said that the early church had to explain why Jesus was not recognized as the Messiah and ultimately was executed, so it read back into the life of Jesus the idea that he kept his claims secret. However, if Mark as editor was so interested in proving his point, why did he leave in Jesus' cure of a paralytic before a crowd (Mark 2:1–12) or of the man with a withered hand in a synagogue (Mark 3:1–6)? If the theory is right, he would have dropped these stories, or have rewritten them in private settings and added secrecy commands.

But what if the Gospels are honest, reliable history—as Christians have believed across the centuries? Does this make Christianity a secretive religion at its core? The modern French Catholic scholars' notes to *The Jerusalem Bible* point out that the Jewish people were looking for a political Messiah to liberate them from Rome, and that Jesus wanted to avoid encouraging this erroneous idea. Some writers say that these stories emphasize the need for a sense of sacredness. Several of the secrecy verses express Jesus' natural desire to avoid the phony adulation of crowds, particularly when it could have hindered his work or even have been dangerous. The secrecy sayings cannot be considered normative in Jesus' ministry, since there were so many examples of public teaching and activity.

More troublesome is Jesus' shrouding of religious truth in parables during public teaching, then explaining the meaning to his disciples later in private, particularly in Mark 4. Yet the Parable of the Lamp in this passage makes clear that the ultimate purpose is to reveal the truths ("nothing kept secret except to be brought to light") to those who had begun to respond to him. Even Jesus' pessimistic quote from Isaiah ("that they . . . may hear and hear again, but not understand") can be understood as a clause of consequence, a realistic recognition that the teachings would inevitably lead to hardened unbelief among many.

As for the New Testament church after Jesus' ascension, the apostles could almost be called publicity-seekers when it came to preaching their beliefs. There is evidence that some of the early church's worship meetings were open to outsiders as a means of evangelism, even though the Christians were then a struggling new group subject to harassment. Paul sought to impose order on tongues-speaking in worship lest those outsiders attending a service "would say you were all mad" (I Corinthians 14:23).

Modern Catholicism teaches unequivocally that its beliefs are a necessary part of the church's self-disclosure to the world. But, remarkably, this has not always been the case. In the era of the Church Fathers secrecy was applied to many of the most important religious materials of Christianity. This phenomenon deserves a close look, because it shows the extent to which secrecy policies have been contextual in church history. If secrecy policies arose on sacred matters, and then waned as circumstances changed, then a shift is certainly legitimate in the less crucial matters of church administration. And since early church secrecy occurred during a time of persecution, it can add to our understanding of how secrecy could be forced upon persecuted churches in our own century.

The early church's *disciplina arcani* (discipline of the secret), which forbade church members to provide information to outsiders on sacred truths and rites, appeared in the second century and waxed strong in the third through the fifth centuries. With the formal organization of a catechumenate preparing for church membership, even these Christians-in-waiting were admitted to knowledge only gradually. At its height, secrecy applied to the baptism and confirmation rites, the Our Father and other worship texts, the Eucharist, and the creeds and Scriptures. The *New Catholic Encyclopedia* states that by the fourth century Christianity had developed "an aura of secrecy."

In the early liturgies the first part of the service consisted of Psalms, Epistles, Gospel readings, and an exhortation or sermon. At this point the non-Christians, catechumens, and penitents were ordered to leave. As the congregation continued with the prayers, creed, and Eucharist, the church doors customarily were locked and guarded to keep the uninitiated from barging in, inadvertently or otherwise. So strict was the custom, according to one historian, that if one of these came in by mistake, he was immediately instructed in the faith and baptized. The two-part structure of the service resulted in some liturgical dislocation, since the Our Father and other materials which would naturally come early in the service were placed later, after the exclusion. The literature of the era reports no use of church laws to enforce the discipline, nor do we have evidence of an oath of secrecy being required from those joining the church. However, the initiation ceremony itself was sometimes conducted during the night to enhance privacy.

The arguments in favor of secrecy by the Church Fathers made little use of Jesus' own sayings. The one exception was his curious statement in Matthew 7:6 against giving holy things to dogs or throwing "pearls in front of pigs." The earliest citation of this text in support of a closed-door Eucharist was in the *Didache,* an anonymous second-century treatise on church order. (Exegetes today agree that "dogs" and "pigs" are terms—very harsh in that historical context— to refer to outsiders.) Among those who accept the saying as historical, it has been explained as advocating a religious sense of reserve and propriety. New Testament historian Floyd Filson, among others, said that it means the Christian should not insist on speaking in hopelessly hostile circumstances. In the second century the Christians made a broad public appeal. The *Shepherd of Hermas* mentioned an open invitation to all to attend Christian meetings (presumably the first part only) and Tatianus specified that all who wished were admitted to instruction.

Tertullian of Carthage was the first of the major fathers to defend secret worship, although his ambiguity may indicate that the practice was not firmly fixed in the late second century. Tertullian boasted in *Ad Nationes* that while the evildoer shrinks from publicity, the Christian is not ashamed, except of former sins. "When questioned, he confesses; when condemned, he rejoices." And ironically, Tertullian elsewhere depended on the assertion that Jesus concealed nothing from the Twelve to refute the Gnostics, the various mystical groups whose moral hatred of the material world caused them to reject the orthodox belief that Christ was God in bodily form. Gnostics claimed access to special knowledge of Jesus through hidden revelations reserved for the initiated. These claims were counteracted by the existence of a widely known and openly distributed body of literature. Thus publicity was central to the formation of a canon of authoritative New Testament documents. As French scholar Jacques Hervieux puts it, the four Gospels presented "a revelation of salvation brought by Christ which was addressed to all men, without mystery or secret cult."

The most detailed Christian discussion in support of sacred secrecy appeared, not coincidentally, in Alexandria, where the faith took on a Gnostic coloration. In his *Stromata* ("Miscellanies"), Clement asserted that "it is requisite . . . to hide in a mystery the wisdom spoken, which the Son of God taught." Though Clement used a few strained interpretations of Scripture, the bulk of his argument came from the history of numerous non-Christian religions, with Judaism rating much less attention than paganism. Accurately enough, he reported that in their religions both Greeks and barbarians "have veiled the first principles of things, and delivered the truth in enigmas, and symbols, and allegories, and metaphors." He particularly honored his Egyptian forebears for their high-powered elitist religion: They "did not entrust the mysteries they possessed to all and sundry, and did not divulge the knowledge of divine things to the profane," but only to the worthiest priests and "those destined to ascend the throne." An echo of this in Christianity's growing distinction between the clergy and laity would help to reinforce secrecy.

It was not surprising that paganism provided Clement with the best support for secrecy. To modern scholars orthodox Christianity's openness was one of its most important contrasts with competing faiths. Millar Burrows notes that the Qumran ("Dead Sea Scrolls") sect was a closed, ultraexclusive community—the extreme opposite of Christianity. Our understanding of the markedly secret style of heretical groups has been broadened with the discovery of the Egyptian Gnostic gospels at Nag-Hammadi. The open fact of a central historical person, and the open proclamation of the message, were significant differences between the mystery religions and Christianity.

Two defenses of Christianity written in Clement's era show the ammunition that secrecy provided the enemies of the religion. In Minucius Felix' *Octavius,* the heathen Caecelius argued as follows in a fictional dialogue with the Christian Octavius: "Why do they endeavor with such pains to conceal and to cloak whatever they worship, since honorable things always rejoice in publicity, while crimes are kept secret? . . . Why do they never speak openly, never congregate freely, unless for the reason that what they adore and conceal is either worthy of punishment or something to be ashamed of?" The author's reply dodged the basic objection, and merely denied all the rumors about Christians practicing sacrilege, incest, adultery, parricide, drunkenness, and ritual infanticide. In Origen's classic *Contra Celsum* we learn that the Greek philsopher Celsus (whose writings are now known to us only through Origen's work) had used charges of illegal secret association as his first point to discredit Christianity. Origen's reply was maladroit. He countered the accusation of illegal secrecy by admitting the charge was true, then justifying such civil disobedience because it was done for the sake of "truth." This work made it obvious that to whatever degree secrecy was then practiced, it was not efficient enough to prevent the Greek Celsus from becoming well-informed on Christian practices.

Christian writing from the third century shows the odd reinterpretations that were made of New Testament personalities in support of secrecy. Bishop Hippolytus of Rome, citing Paul's admonitions to Timothy on safeguarding the faith, commented, "How much greater will be our danger if, rashly and without thought, we commit the revelations of God to profane and unworthy men?" What Paul in fact did was to provide repeated instructions for spreading the beliefs which he had already proclaimed in public—and at no small danger to himself. By the third century such caution had arisen that he was cited to prevent non-Christian ears from hearing those beliefs!

Stranger yet, the treatise *Recognitiones,* conventionally ascribed to Clement of Rome, put the ubiquitous "pearls in front of pigs" verse in the mouth of St. Peter, and then had the Fisherman add: "Nothing is more difficult, my brethren, than to reason concerning the truth in the presence of a mixed multitude of poeple." If a Christian sets forth "pure truth to those who do not desire to obtain salvation, he does injury" to Christ. "I also, for the most part, by using a certain circumlocution, endeavor to avoid publishing the chief knowledge concerning the Supreme Divinity to unworthy ears." The writer could hardly have chosen a more inappropriate figure to speak those words, in the light of Peter's hotblooded public preaching career beginning at Pentecost. There Peter began Christianity's first sermon, "Men of Judaea, and all you who live in Jerusalem. . . ."

The fourth century sermons such as those of St. John Chrysostom were dotted with evasions and phrases such as "the initiated know what we say." Because the unbaptized were present, the preachers felt compelled to be obscure on such matters as the Trinity, Incarnation, creeds, and texts. St. Jerome mentioned the practice of keeping the Trinity and Incarnation as secrets from adult catechumens until about forty days before their baptism—and this after two to three years of instruction. In one of his sermons St. Augustine of Hippo stated that only baptism and the Eucharist were secret, but elsewhere he noted that catechumens did not hear the Our Father until seven days before baptism. Joseph Bingham, a thorough if rather polemical nineteenth-century historian, stated that Sozomen kept a creedal text out of his fifth-century church history because creeds were secret. Bingham also said that Roman Catholicism supported the idea that the early church believed in transubstantiation and seven sacraments, for which there is no documentation, on the argument that such practices were secret so there was no written evidence. Obviously, the search for reliable church history in these distant centuries is greatly hindered insofar as secrecy prevented the patristic writers from recording their beliefs and practices.

Why did secrecy about belief become so entrenched? An explanation developed in the nineteenth century, which still has its adherents today, was that the early church modeled its practices on those of the pagan mystery religions, and certainly Clement of Alexandria provides support for this idea. More recent historians suggest that converts accustomed to the more elaborate Jewish or pagan rites might have been put off by the simplicity of the Christian practices until they had had an opportunity to understand their meaning. Presumably secrecy also encouraged reverence for the mysteries, and helped preserve the dignity of worship. Another possibility is that heathen converts needed preparation so their curiosity and ignorance would not lead to extreme irreverence, or that those raised in idolatry and fetishism needed careful instruction to understand the proper meaning of the Eucharist or the Trinity. The most extreme theory would be that secrecy was used to excite curiosity and zeal among the catechumens. The most plausible explanation, however, is that secrecy was simply a product of a persecuted "ghetto" church with a strong sense of separation from evil and pagan surroundings. In that era Christians tended toward a general spirit of withdrawal from the culture. They avoided not only immoral practices, but common amusements, education, and government and military service. In everyday life this cultural withdrawal may have been far more important than any of the theological justifications.

Persecution of the early church also had a reciprocal relationship with secrecy, although it is difficult to tell which caused which. Lactantius, the noted patristic historian of persecution, provides this revealing passage:

> We are not accustomed to defend and assert [such matters as the end of the world, the Resurrection, and the Last Judgment] in public, since God orders in quietness and silence to hide his secret, and to keep it within our own conscience; and not to strive with obstinate contention against those who are ignorant of the truth. . . . For a mystery ought to be most faithfully concealed and covered, especially by us who bear the name of faith. But they accuse this silence of ours, as though it were the result of an evil conscience; whence also they invent some detestable things respecting those who are holy and blameless, and willingly believe their own inventions.

Some historians say it is probable that persecution arose out of misconceptions that both educated and uneducated people received of Christian practices. Lacking direct proof, the heathens believed that the Christians practiced immoral rites. Tertullian defended the Christians against charges that they were atheists (showing public misinformation) and cannibals (presumably a misinterpretation of the Eucharist). Septimius Severus was favorable toward the Christians when he became emperor in A.D. 193, but he later enforced severe laws against secret societies. Many Christians were harassed or executed because they were members of such an organization. Along with such overt troubles with the non-Christian society, the Church Fathers indicate that lingering resentment also resulted, and the appeal of Christianity must certainly have been weakened by it.

The secrecy discipline arose in the postapostolic period when persecution began to be a problem, and it eventually died out after Constantine gave Christianity legal standing in the empire. After this, the Christians gradually decided that they were no longer a beleaguered band which had to preserve its faith from intrusion. If irreverence or atrocities had contributed to the rise of the discipline, the church could now depend on the state to protect it, rather than to join in the persecution. But the heritage of secrecy in belief, which departed radically from the practice of the original apostles, probably influenced the church's practice on far less important matters, both in the church's relation to the world and in church leaders' relation to their own constituency.

Secrecy in ritual and belief developed under special circumstances after the New Testament period, and has long since disappeared. It was produced less by Christian tradition than by a strange combination of respect for the secret practices in paganism, on the one hand, and fear of pagan culture on the other. The lack of Scriptural support indicates that such secrecy is not intrinsic to Christianity.

Although persecution was a major cause of early forms of secrecy, persecution in the twentieth century has produced a much different reaction. Christians today are open about their beliefs, even when self-protection—or even survival—requires secrecy on other aspects of church life. Just as secrecy about beliefs is not "normal" for Christians, so other secrecy policies under persecution must be considered as reactions to emergency situations. Under Nazism, Fascism, Communism, or in localized areas in nontotalitarian societies, the church often has found it necessary to conceal membership lists, location of services, and information about finances and activities. Church leaders have had to hide their plans not only from hostile outsiders but from their own members. It would be ill-advised for most church groups to follow the administrative secrecy used by persecuted Catholics in Reformation England, or by Nazi Germany's "Confessing Church," or by the current "Initiative" Baptist movement in the Soviet Union, just as it would be ill-advised for the modern church to follow the clubbish concealment of beliefs that characterized parts of the early church.

The current debate on Catholic secrecy in the West does not deal with ritual or dogma, but with more mundane matters of administration, and with the flow of information about it to church members and to outsiders with a legitimate interest. Secrecy on sacred matters has become a mere curiosity of history, but it doubtless had an effect on the development of other types of secrecy in the succeeding centuries of church history.

6 The Open Centuries

Secrecy is so omnipresent in the administration of the Catholic church that it might seem to have existed since the year 1. Surprisingly, history records something quite different. The church was born in openness, and only gradually developed a culture of secretive administration. As late as the Reformation the church allowed considerable freedom of information. Only in modern times and particularly the nineteenth century, described in the next chapter, did secrecy gain a stranglehold, causing the anachronistic survival of such practices in our own time.

Because power begets information, and information begets power, the development of secrecy can be traced generally through the participation of the membership at large in church decision-making. The following account, obviously not a thorough history of the question, sketches some of the major developments between the openness of the New Testament and the church's latter-day secrecy. Although the story emphasizes the information barriers between clergy and laity, it should be remembered that there are also barriers today between priest and priest, between bishop and priest, between bishop and bishop, between dioceses and religious orders, and (the latest wrinkle) between the new conservative and liberal organizations and the church establishment.

The spread of information in the twentieth century, with modern mass media, is vastly different from what it was in the century when Christianity was born. We cannot state with certainty that all the information in the New Testament was available in its own time to all church members, or to outsiders in an environment that was very hostile to the new faith. But we do observe within the church a spirit of sharing. We can assume that relevant information was necessarily available to all members because the Christian community clearly was meant to consist of knowledgeable, responsible individuals.

In terms of church government the precedent was set at the Council of Jerusalem (approximately A.D. 51), the most important meeting of the apostolic church. The church's first council is described in Acts 15, and the apparent existence of St. Paul's "insider's" account of the same meeting in Galatians 2 underscores the importance of the event. The entire Christian community of Jerusalem participated. The general membership welcomed Paul and Barnabas to town, a large group listened to all or part of the crucial policy debate on whether to insist on the Jewish law, and the envoys sent to Antioch were elected by the entire community. Yves Congar in *Lay People in the Church* (1965) notes that the final decision-making power at the council rested with the apostles and elders, not the entire company, but the decision-makers saw no need to keep the information from the people, nor to bar the people from expressing their opinions for consideration by the leaders. In this way they had a definite part in the decision.

John McKenzie's important discussion in *Authority in the Church* (1966) says that when Luke described this council making a major decision by common consent after open deliberation, he obviously did not consider this something extraordinary in church practice. Nor did this style of decision-making weaken the necessary authority and force of the decision, once it had been reached. And how were the leaders other than the apostles selected? The choosing of the Seven (Acts 6:5) indicates that election by the whole church was the way leadership offices were to be filled. This shared authority was only natural, says McKenzie, because the mission of the church in spreading the Gospel was the responsibility of all the members. McKenzie remarks that modern church "over-management" is "a vote of non-confidence in the ability of the members of the Church to fulfill their own office." It is as though the church no longer has the ability to produce a number of people with the ability to make plans and carry them out without constant, detailed direction from an ecclesiastical officer. "Paul had no doubt that the Apostolic Church had this power. What has the Church lost since apostolic times?" It seems that the renewed Catholic interest in biblical evidence must inevitably lead the church toward the open apostolic style.

During the first centuries after New Testament times the functions performed by the laity gradually became centralized in the offices of priest and bishop. For instance, in the first two centuries lay persons could preach if no bishop was present or, later on, if no clergyman was present. Eventually they lost the right to preach. Under certain circumstances, in the first two centuries the laity also conducted baptism and the Eucharist (though Ignatius issued a mild reproof of the latter in an epistle). Historian Edwin Hatch wrote in 1918 that the common body of administrative officers in the early church evolved into concentration in a single bishop. By the time of Justin Martyr charity offerings went to the presiding officer of the assembly rather than directly to the needy, and money became an important component of authority. Hatch said that the *episcopos* (bishop) was a financial officer in secular terminology, and that the centralization of financial power had much to do with the development of a church hierarchy—not the reverse. Other historians said that the *episcopos* was an overseer of all sorts of affairs and the term did not necessarily refer to financial administration. In either case, it is significant that these overseers were originally *elected* by the entire Christian community. Even after the bishops assumed financial control, however, the laity continued to have an important role in day-to-day administration. The African churches of the third and fourth centuries had *seniores laici,* most likely elected by the people, who joined in management and served as judges in church courts. However, as Yves Congar pointed out, the priesthood made a concerted move in the fourth and fifth centuries to take management of temporal goods away from the laity.

Bingham's detailed account of the early bishop's role in money management contrasts with current practice. In the fourth and fifth centuries all revenues were in the hands of the bishop, distributed with the advice and consent of a priests' senate. To avoid suspicion and to prevent mismanagement the bishop was required to give an account of his fiscal administration to the synod of his province. When a man was elected bishop, he had to exhibit a public list of his own possessions to distinguish them from those of the church.

Nevertheless, corruption was persistent. The Council of Chalcedon (A.D. 451) ordered each bishop to have an *oeconomus* (guardian), chosen by a vote of all the clergy, to manage diocesan revenues under the inspection of the bishop. One reason was the bishop's pressing spiritual duties due to the large-scale conversion of the heathen. But corruption was another reason, since the acts of the Council of Tyre (A.D. 448) mention embezzlement charges against two bishops. Although all the *oeconomi* were clergymen, so far as we can tell, Chalcedon's purpose was to have "witnesses" to proper administration, which obviously meant the witness of probity was made to the whole Christian community. The *oeconomus* retained his office when the bishop's seat was vacant, and he kept things in hand for the new bishop (perhaps to prevent the metropolitan of the region from enriching his own funds out of the diocesan treasury!). Considerable sums were involved. In Chrysostom's time 3,000 persons were on the church welfare rolls in Antioch alone. The Fifth Council of Carthage (A.D. 401) required the bishop to consult with his clergy, as well as with the metropolitan, before selling specified church goods.

Hatch analyzed the centralization of church power over the centuries as follows: Christianity grew to become an extensive enterprise, and a general centralization was only natural. After Constantine in-

fant baptism and broad community membership led to a variety of
levels of conviction and moral standards among the church membership, so that a separate, higher criterion came to be used for officers
and the clergy class became more distinct. State recognition also
meant that the church could hold property. The clergy became a
favored, monied class when they were set apart from civic duties and
taxation and received a regular salary from the state. Early monasti-
cism and Montanism were examples of the various protests against
centralization and affluence, which became ever stronger once the
church became part of the Establishment. This class system gradually
affected all areas of church life, presumably including information on
finances and other matters.

Beyond the questions of money the laity in the early church had
an important role in setting church policy. One of the most significant
texts demonstrating this is a letter to priests and deacons in A.D. 250
from Bishop Cyprian, a key figure in the development of Catholic
ecclesiology because of his high view of the See of Rome. In the letter
Cyprian explained that he had not replied to Donatus and his other
enemies unilaterally because "from the beginning of my episcopate,
I decided to do nothing of my own opinion privately without *your
advice and the consent of the people.*" This important bishop stated
that all church members should be informed of policy matters in
advance of a decision, and must give their consent. Although a later
African bishop, Augustine of Hippo, insisted on the secrecy discipline
for the sacraments, his sermons notified the people about even minor
church matters, including the sort of disputes and scandals that would
rarely, if ever, be aired today.

Laymen participated in important policy matters at the early
church councils, where there was no pattern of attendance exclusively
by bishops. At an early council in Carthage (A.D. 256) the laity were
not consulted on the question of heretical baptism by bishops, but they
did have a strong voice on whether to readmit lapsed Christians to
fellowship. Deacons and laymen attended the Synod of Elvira (A.D.

305), although they did not sign the acts. At the first Ecumenical Council at Nicaea in A.D. 325 Athanasius, then only a deacon, was a major personality in the debate, and the Arians were even able to get the floor for pagan philosophers to testify. Although laymen were not directly involved, the as-yet-unbaptized Emperor Constantine, of course, played a key role in steering the proceedings. From then on secular rulers were to participate significantly in councils. Since most of these were church members, this could be called a form of lay participation, but involvement of the political elite does not mean sharing of information with the laity in general.

Openness and participation also marked the selection of bishops in the early church. Bishop Cyprian, who wrote more about this than other patristic figures, said, "It comes from divine authority that a bishop be chosen in the presence of the people before the eyes of all, and that he be approved as worthy and fit by public judgment and testimony." He also said that "the suffrage and judgment of all" should be involved in ordination of priests, so that the choice would be just and that "either the crimes of the evildoers may be revealed or the merits of the good may be proclaimed."

In a paper in the Canon Law Society of America's *The Choosing of Bishops* (1971) Thomas F. O'Meara traced in detail how this early practice of bishop selection disappeared. He said that the popular selection mentioned by Cyprian or Pope Gregory the Great was not democratic election as such, but the involvement of the various elements, including all the clergy of the city, and the bishops of the area, with the collective will of the community playing a central role with possible veto power. The pope did not enter the bishop selection process outside of Italy until the end of the first millennium. The laity eventually lost its role altogether, due to social chaos and the corrupting involvement of secular rulers in the appointments. Thus the church at large lost its access to information about the choice of its leaders, and lost also the opportunity of providing its own opinions as part of the information used in making decisions.

By the beginning of the Middle Ages the patterns of hierarchy and secrecy had begun to be set. The problem was exaggerated by the conditions of the day, and social ferment doubtless contributed to defensiveness in many situations. The feudal system had a marked influence on the development of a powerful clergy caste in league with secular powers, both of which were remote from the people. The influence of secular nobles in the church, which had begun with Constantine, reached a high point with the scandals of "lay proprietorship" and "lay investiture," in which local lords owned churches and appointed priests. Candidates for desirable parishes, and even bishoprics, bought their positions or gave pledges of political support. These worldly bishops and priests were often more loyal to the princes than to the popes. Thus lay power came to be identified with corruption in the church, and reform movements arose to regain pure clergy control. This partially explains the church's distrust of lay involvement in subsequent centuries.

Not all the involvement of nonbishops in the medieval church councils consisted of the nobility. There is evidence of the presence of laymen and the lower clergy from the fifth century on, in Rome, Spain, and the French and Germanic areas. Laymen were asked to attend the Council of Toledo (A.D. 633), for example, so that they could be informed about abuses. The monastic orders, which had lay origins, gained a strong voice at the Sixth Ecumenical Council (Constantinople, A.D. 680), and the seventh (Nicaea, A.D. 787) was convoked and in part presided over by a laywoman, the Empress Irene. In the eleventh century Pope Gregory VII wanted to call a synod fully representing the clergy and laity, but the investiture dispute frustrated his plan. The chronicle of a papal synod in A.D. 1095 reported that more than 30,000 laity and 4,000 clergy were present, and that the session had to be held in an open field. The pope consciously used broad lay representation at one council to help drum up support for the Crusades. Records from the various councils at the Lateran and Lyons show participation by the Templars, a delegation of Waldensians, secular authorities, and laymen named as representatives.

The papal chaos over the Great Schism meant that the Council of Constance (1414–1418), which tried to unify the church, sought broad representation from the community at large. At the height of the proceedings there were 215 hierarchs, 150 abbots and priors, nearly 300 doctors of theology, and a retinue of clergy and other advisers, which brought total attendance to about 18,000. Full voting rights were granted to the theologians, canonists, and important laymen. At the later, radical Council of Basel, bishops formed less than a tenth of the participants.

Despite the defensive task set before the Council of Trent, or perhaps because of it, lay participation was noteworthy. Noblemen attended, a layman preached one of the sermons, and the council's secretary was a layman. The right to vote was limited much more than at the fifteenth-century councils. Nevertheless, as described in a paper by Jose Luis Martin-Descaloza, contemporary records of Trent tell of people going in and out of sessions, and the discussions of problems showed that censorship was not practiced. Pope Pius IV favored freedom of expression in the council, and even his fear that discord would strengthen the hand of heretics did not cause him to require secrecy. Martin-Descaloza says that "all those who write letters or send reports from Trent do it in a natural way which supposes an absolute freedom of information. They never seem to worry about what they say or do not say about discussions or decrees. The letters from the bishop of Lérida, from Lainez and other theologians, are an authentic mine of press information."

However, in church judicial proceedings, notably the inquisitions, secrecy was used skillfully by the hierarchy. Historian A. S. Turberville said in *Medieval Heresy and the Inquisition* (1920) that the tight secrecy imposed on all the proceedings greatly hampered the defendants, as was true of the operations of the "Holy Office" in later centuries. "There was none of the security that comes from an open trial, none of the encouragement to make a good fight for freedom, for honour, for life, that comes from publicity." The defense also faced the fact that the names of the accusers were customarily kept secret. This custom began when the inquisitions faced an unfriendly populace, and witnesses took a risk in providing evidence of heresy. As things later developed it was the defendant, not the prosecution witnesses, who had an urgent need of protection against an unfriendly public. It could be argued that in certain hysterical settings the secrecy of hearings was a protection against mob action. Church officialdom sometimes made strategic use of publicity to put pressure on the state. For example, a clergy-led clamor of public opinion brought about the conviction of Marechal Gilles de Rais, a Frenchman who had had children slain and used their blood to write a book on the necromantic arts.

By the late Middle Ages the laity had lost its original voice in church affairs, and its access to information, except for the nobility. But church affairs and political affairs were intertwined, and secrecy was not so much a matter of policy as the way things tended to operate in a hierarchical church and state. It was later developments—the printing press, the Protestant revolt, skepticism and anticlericalism, the demise of the Papal States, the persecution of the Catholic church —that produced a widespread and conscious policy of secrecy that is still in evidence today.

7 Drawing the Curtain

"For at least the first sixteen centuries there was fluent news and a true, vital participation of the community," concluded John A. Lee in his research on Vatican communications. This means, he said, that "open doors and information are clearly the historical tradition," even though the church has distinguished the functions of the hierarchy from those of other Catholics. The cover-up in major church meetings, in the handling of everyday affairs, and in the selection of church leaders is a modern development.

It started, perhaps, with the discovery of the printing press and the beginnings of mass culture. The Catholic church sought new controls on the flow of information because the press could become a means for the unprecedented spread of theological and moral error. The growth of Protestantism, in particular, depended upon the printing press because the new schismatics emphasized mass reading of the Bible and a rational verbalized theology in which each layman was to participate.

By the nineteenth century, when secrecy reached its height, Catholicism had suffered centuries of Protestant incursion and resulting persecution, then the ravages of skepticism, which had led to severe repression of the church in France. The powerful Masons were campaigning against Catholicism. New scientific and intellectual developments seemed to threaten the foundations of the faith.

Besides that, the papacy was influenced by the fact that the pope had long been a secular prince, ruling the Papal States. While Western countries were moving from the controlled press of the monarchical age toward the beginnings of the modern news media, the Papal States were still autocratic in their political system. The Vatican's absolutist, medieval style of secular government, including oppressive press censorship, was transferred naturally into the administration of the church.

The war of nerves between the Vatican and the printing press began as early as 1515, two years before Luther's "95 Theses" sparked the Reformation. In that year Pope Leo X spoke of the press as a form of progress, but he was also worried that it would be used to spread errors. Later in that century the first systematic press censorship developed. One element in this was a controversial form of journalism that cropped up in the Italian states. The *avvisi* ("advices" on what was happening), first handwritten and later printed, were gossip sheets, the forerunners of the more reputable modern newspaper. The *avvisi* proved that men always desire and need information, and that communications media will develop to meet this demand—whether reliable or unreliable, establishmentarian or "underground."

Naturally enough, the *avvisi* took a particular interest in the Vatican and spread many grisly tidbits about life there. Maria Luisa Ambrosini reports that possession of *avvisi* was made illegal, and by 1571 Pope Pius V officially forbade Christians to write them. A harsher decree from Pope Gregory XIII (1572–1585) said, "There has recently appeared a new sect of men illicitly curious, who write every kind of information of which they have knowledge, or which they make up out of their own libidinous imaginations, mixing the false, the true, and the uncertain with no restraint whatever." The penalties for writing or disseminating these papers were perpetual infamy, imprisonment, or hanging. Under Pope Sixtus V (1585–1590), at least one of these protojournalists was dismembered. Even writers of straightforward news were considered criminals. By the seventeenth century the Roman government, in effect, permitted journalism by ordering that *avvisi* not be written without the permission of secular officials, with death as the punishment for any libelous material. But, writes Ambrosini, "the new profession was on its way to being securely established. The Papal States, beginning their long decline, had good reason to fear it."

The Vatican's antipress attitude had escalated considerably by 1814, when Pope Pius VII wrote a complaint to Louis XVIII about the recognition of freedom of the press in France's new constitution. The pope said that press freedom was "the principal instrument which has, first, depraved the morals of the people, then corrupted and destroyed their faith, and finally, stirred up seditions, troubles, and revolts. These unfortunate results are now still to be feared, considering the great malice of men, if (God forbid) everyone were given the liberty to print whatever he pleased." An encyclical from Pope Gregory XVI in 1832 called liberty of conscience a "most pestilential error" and condemned "that worst and never sufficiently to be execrated and detested liberty of the press." The most famous example of this mindset was the *Syllabus of Errors*, a catalogue of 80 condemned ideas that Pope Pius IX attached to an encyclical in 1864. The last point was that the pope cannot reconcile himself to "progress, liberalism, and modern civilization."

Pius' position had hardened when his political regime came under attack in the Italian Revolution, which was anti-church in tone. In the years after 1848 Pius had had to flee Rome, and his political fortunes worsened at the same time that rationalism was growing among Europe's intellectuals. The democratic press quite naturally played a role in the assault on the Vatican oligarchy. The Vatican in turn banned the secular press for a time in the Papal States and created its own organ of defense, the newspaper *L'Osservatore Romano.*

All these antagonisms reached their height during Vatican Council I, which had to be adjourned abruptly because of the attacks on the Papal States. In this unusual setting self-disclosure by the Vatican reached an all-time low. Vatican I was the first wholly and officially secret Ecumenical Council in history and the first without significant lay representation. In fact, the laity were expressly forbidden to attend the proceedings, except for liturgical occasions. This meant the broad Christian community depended on secondary sources for its only participation. Yet even this sort of contact was made nearly impossible by a rigidly enforced oath of secrecy inside the council.

Journalism had not existed during the previous council, Trent, so no attempt was made, or could be, to inform the public on a daily basis. Vatican I opened new opportunities for church public relations. However, through much of the century the press, especially in Italy and France, had distorted and often ridiculed the Catholic church. The few newspapermen at the council got no cooperation and had to depend on Vatican tipsters. As Christopher Butler's history of the council noted, the press detested the "thick veil of secrecy" and was "altogether hostile" for the most part.

The secrecy problems actually began well before the council even opened. The Vatican court kept strict secrecy over council preparations, withholding information even from many bishops. Some of the outsiders sensed a conspiracy to formulate an agenda for railroading through certain views in the *Syllabus* and an extreme stance on papal powers, before effective opposition could be prepared.

One curious episode involved Augustin Theiner, the prefect of the Secret Archives. Theiner had been given permission to publish the documents from the Council of Trent, and had been at work on them since 1857. In 1870 Pope Pius IX gave strict orders to Theiner not to show the Trent documents to any member of the Catholic hierarchy, apparently fearing that knowledge of the previous council's procedures would prove detrimental to his own plans. However, a copy of the order of business at Trent somehow leaked out, and the minority Germans made use of it in opposing the Curia schemes. The pope immediately fired Theiner, who died an outcast four years later.

As the council opened, the secrecy gave unusual impact to the

"Roman Letters" which appeared in the press under the pseudonym of Quirinius. They constituted a polemical attack on the council, seeking to discredit its decisions before they had even been made. Yet these letters were the only detailed account available of what was happening during the council's first months. Whatever their biases, the letters seemed to be based upon firsthand knowledge. The success of the letters among the Catholic faithful can be explained only by the lid of secrecy which made them so essential, and so intriguing.

Meanwhile, several members of the minority which opposed papal infallibility leaked strategic information to diplomats or their influential friends. The bishops came to distrust the seminarians who worked as council stenographers. Two Curia prelates were fired because documents were lost, and the Vatican police even imprisoned the secretary of an Armenian bishop for a similar offense. Although the pope prohibited all publication regarding the council, he later personally authorized certain bishops to make known matters which were useful for his side. The council majority gradually began leaking material to trusted newsmen.

On all sides, then, the press was manipulated with selective, propagandistic information on the council. The barriers led to abnormal efforts to influence the proceedings, such as a barrage of editorials and letters to the editor, and one gathering of laymen in Rome which sought to bring outside pressure. Inside the council a considerable amount of the limited time was spent debating the press and information problems. The secrecy policy, of course, did not work. Information on the council was rife, but it was necessarily a mix of truth and rumor. None of the clergy and laity of the church could be at all sure what was going on and why. The atmosphere of distrust could not be dispelled, since the bishops refused even to publish their own bulletin of the proceedings. Historians of the council agree that the secrecy tactic was utterly disastrous.

The spirit and precedents of Vatican I could do nothing but reinforce the strong tendencies toward secrecy at all levels of Catholicism, down to the diocese and the parish. Meanwhile, the development of the Curia, the high view of the papacy, and a form of priestly triumphalism in reaction to anticlericalism continued to diminish the role of the laity in church affairs and, with it, the church's perception of the laity's right to church information. The nineteenth century still has great influence on the style of the church. Under severe pressure the church is tempted to distort its internal policies. And just as the early Christians formed a "ghetto church" that was secretive on sacred matters, while more open in administration, the defensive church after the fall of the Papal States created a political ghetto for itself. Even in more recent times the bishops and clergy often have reflected an insular spirit and a feeling of anxiety toward outsiders. Meanwhile, the laity assumed a docile role in church affairs.

At the Vatican the results of this mentality were typified in 1903 when reporters covering the terminal illness of Pope Leo XIII ran into a blank wall of secrecy on Leo's condition. All dispatches from the Vatican had to be cleared through a censor, much like what reporters faced for decades in Moscow. One enterprising French newsman decided to send a daily cable saying "POPE DEAD." If Leo was still alive, he figured, the censor would kill the cable, but if it was true he would let it pass and the reporter would have a worldwide scoop. But the censor got tired of the game after several days and let the cable through even though the pope was still alive, so Leo "died" in the Paris newspapers two weeks prematurely.

In the United States the Catholic church had a special style of provincialism during the nineteenth century. The succeeding waves of immigrants faced hostility or persecution from many in the Protestant majority. Due to these outside pressures the Catholic community was largely ghettoized. Besides this, the church was led by many Irish immigrants who associated the "secular" press with the papers they had known in Ireland, which were part of the hated English Protestant establishment. Because of the strident, often-partisan American journalism in those days, the U.S. bishops became frozen in an attitude that the press was hostile to Catholicism. Vestiges of this view survive today, long after conditions have changed for the better.

The early pattern of church administration in the U.S. reflected some of the democratic spirit of the nation. From the beginning a council of parish laymen often held title to the church property. But "lay trusteeship" became a bitter problem when the laity also claimed that they had a right to call and dismiss their own priests, Protestant-style, without the bishop's approval. The first bishop of Charleston, South Carolina, John England, solved the trusteeship problem with a diocesan constitution that gave him final control over property, with finances administered by a board of six priests and twelve elected laymen. An annual convention of clergy and elected lay delegates was set up to scrutinize the work of the church, but the bishop retained the authority to take action. John Cogley in *Catholic America (1973)* writes that England's successors abolished this operation, and that largely because of the trusteeship hassle "for generations every proposal to enlarge the role of the laity in ecclesiastical affairs was rejected out of hand."

By today's standards it is remarkable that Pope Pius VI granted the nation's priests the power to elect their first bishop, John Carroll, in 1789. However, when it came time to choose Carroll's coadjutor the Vatican ruled out an election, even though it acknowledged that a direct appointment from Rome would be interpreted by anti-Catholics as a violation of the spirit of the U.S. Constitution. So Carroll was advised to consult with his older priests, with the promise that the pope would appoint Carroll's choice. Carroll, however, called an election by the priests as his form of consultation. But by 1807, notes historian Robert Trisco, the priests had lost their vote. Carroll apparently proposed appointees for the new sees of Boston, Philadelphia, and Bardstown, Kentucky, without consulting the clergy. And the Vatican, without consulting Carroll, named an Irishman living in Rome as the first bishop of New York.

A decree drafted for the U.S. bishops' Second Plenary Council after the Civil War asked that counselors to bishops be permitted to express opinions on episcopal candidates, but this inclusion of a coterie of favorites did not meet the demand of priests who wanted wider consultation, and the Vatican turned down the proposal. The bishops themselves killed another proposal which recommended publication of the names of candidates. The original document had argued that "what is sometimes unknown by many is known by a few, and thus in a way even the people's opinion may be sought out in a matter which is of very great importance to them." But a committee of theologians at the council opposed public discussion of the candidates' merits, fearing rivalries among different ethnic groups. And the Vatican, in rejecting even limited consultation, said such a procedure would work against secrecy, which was considered necessary to avoid arousing unseemly ambition in priests.

The issue persisted. In 1878 Bishop George Conroy, the temporary apostolic delegate to Canada, reported to the Vatican after an intensive tour of the U.S. on the discontent he found among the clergy. Selection of bishops was one of the two major grievances, and Conroy said "since the bishops observe secrecy regarding the [names] that they have proposed to the Holy See, any communication of information about the demerits of the candidate, if he should have any, is rendered impossible."

The U.S. bishops' Third Plenary Council (1884) set up a new system in which all parish rectors with ten years' experience assembled and submitted three names to the bishops of the province. After Vatican approval this system was used until 1916, when the requirement of consultation with priests was eliminated. The reasons for this retrenchment, Trisco reports, were political struggles over vacant sees, and frequent violations of the secrecy rule by priests who participated. In 1910 the Vatican issued a decree which argued that candidates whose names became known were often subjected to unjust public discussion, and that the Holy See's judgment and freedom of choice were hindered. Therefore, those consulted were put under a strict oath of secrecy.

Under the 1916 plan bishops were to ask veteran pastors and diocesan consultors individually (not at a meeting) to suggest one name apiece, although the bishops were under no obligation to follow this advice. The result was the virtual elimination of a formal role of priests in the process. The Holy See worked from the end of Vatican Council II to 1972, preparing a new list of norms for proposing candidates. Under the new, slightly liberalized rules consultation with individual priests or laity is recommended, and the national bishops' conference is given a role along with the pope's resident diplomat. Strict secrecy is required throughout the process.

The degree of consultation remains far less than that proposed by the Canon Law Society of America in 1971. The canonists called for "the broadest participation of the whole People of God" in determining qualifications for bishops and in proposing names, to be conducted by a committee chosen by the diocesan pastoral council or priests' senate. The proposal specifies that the committee inform all those it has consulted on which names it sends to the priests' senate. And the priests' senate is to report to the committee concerning the names it has given the diocesan bishop to transmit to the bishops of the province. Raymond Goedert, chairman of the canonists' committee on selection of bishops, remarked that such open accountability "does not remove altogether the possibility of electioneering. But since the number of candidates at [the diocesan] level is still quite large, the danger of undue publicity and politicking seems remote. Moreover, experience has shown us that the alternative of complete secrecy involves inherent dangers which sometimes prove to be a greater risk."

In a revealing parallel to the Western Catholic development, Eastern Orthodoxy has also moved gradually from wide consultation in the election of its bishops toward more centralization. When Christianity became the state religion, says Orthodox scholar John Meyendorff, the lower clergy and laity gradually lost their right to participate, while the secular government has interfered in the process even though this is forbidden by canon law. Meyendorff says that his own

Orthodox Church in America (the former Russian "Metropolia," which has 450 parishes) is practically the only Eastern communion that has returned to the original canonical system, in which candidates are nominated by diocesan assemblies and elected and consecrated by the other bishops.

Changes in the way Catholic bishops are chosen seem remote. A more immediate issue is the blooming of new consultative bodies in the church since Vatican Council II, such as parish and diocesan councils, priests' senates, and advisory groups on a national basis. Any meaningful consultative role for priests and laity involved in such bodies requires their right to know about church affairs. And if they seek to represent the people of God more broadly, then the wider constituency also has a right to know. The new councils have become commonplace but they are by no means universal, and conservatives argue that they have no authority. The Netherlands, which like the U.S. and Canada has a long democratic tradition, has experimented with a nationwide Pastoral Council where bishops, priests, laity, and even some Protestants and non-Christians openly debate church issues. However, the Vatican insists that such meetings have no valid canonical role in Catholicism, and the future of the Dutch meetings, and of the proposal to have a Pastoral Council in the U.S., is in doubt.

Many bishops today, accustomed to one special style of the episcopacy, assume that such wider participation of the membership means a surrender of episcopal government. But as Yves Congar pointed out, the laity of the early church were not judges of doctrine. Still they provided valuable information and advice as part of the leaders' decision-making process. And after the decisions were made, they provided consent and publicity. Administrative secrecy as now practiced is a relatively recent development, conditioned by historical forces. It arose in periods of identifiable crisis, and new circumstances warrant a fresh look at these policies, particularly when there are abundant earlier precedents for openness and so little basis for the practices in Scripture and much of tradition. One aspect of the Catholic secrecy tradition, however, has been constant through the centuries and is unlikely to change in the future: the emphasis on the right to personal privacy.

8 The Right to Privacy

Most of the Catholic teaching on secrecy has dealt with personal and pastoral affairs rather than with the administration of institutions. In this individualistic teaching privacy—and hence secrecy—is considered a virtue. As the average person uses the word, a "secret" is information that is withheld, and the concealment may or may not be justifiable. On the other hand, traditional moral theology tends to use the term in such a way that all secrets are just, by definition. This means that all breaking of secrets is illicit, also by definition. As the discussion proceeds, most moral theologians admit circumstances where secrets should be broken, but the starting bias is pro-secrecy. The problem comes when this abstract view of the protection of individuals unconsciously carries over to Catholic views on the self-protection of institutions in concrete historical situations, which is a far different matter.

In supporting the individual's right to privacy, Catholicism is true to its understanding of the nature of man. This Catholic emphasis is of particular value in a culture like that of America which is little attuned to the importance of privacy. For instance, "liberal" students in the revolt at Columbia University had no ethical hesitations about rifling, reading, and publicizing the private correspondence of the school president. Even a President of the United States, Richard Nixon, is reported to have wiretapped his own brother. Ultimate self-exposure has come to be equated with "honesty," so that the tasteless revelation of personal matters, once the hallmark of Hollywood starlets, has been practiced by prominent clergymen. The Loud family of California won a sort of immortality by permitting a TV crew to record their lives for months on end to produce the series "An American Family."

For those who do not choose to engage in self-exposure there are others willing to do the exposing. Perhaps the interests of history justify such cases as the accounts of the sexual misadventures of the late theologian Paul Tillich written by his widow. But the living as well as the dead were subjected to amateur, arm's-length psychoanalysis in a book on the Kennedy family by Nancy Gager Clinch of the Center for Women Policy Studies. Alexander and Juliette George said that this project was not "psycho-history," but "psycho-McCarthyism." In a *New York Times Magazine* piece Anne Roiphe made a young woman's irregular menstrual periods and adolescent letters matters for mass consumption in an effort to psychologize about why she had become a Fundamentalist. Such performances go well beyond legitimate interest in relevant personal aspects of public figures.

Writing in *U.S. Catholic*, Michael Kennedy attacked the American myths that "total openness" is always necessary, that "open" is a synonym for "honest," and that "the total baring of one's inmost thoughts is always a good." Kennedy said that almost any priest or counselor has seen the victims of the "total openness" cult, refugees from sensitivity sessions, "stripped of all their defenses and psychologically and spiritually naked." "To abolish all secrets, or to treat confidentiality too lightly, presumes that information by itself is a kind of panacea. Yet, as a people, we have never been better informed, and Utopia is still a few years away." In fact, "our emotional and spiritual security, tenuous at best for most people, is in danger of being dissolved. An environment without trust must surely follow. 1984 would arrive in an orgy of openness."

The culture affects what is defined as "private." As Walter Lippmann observed, the affairs of corporations were once considered as private as a man's theology is these days; in an earlier era, a man's theology was a matter of public interest. Whatever the particular social rules, man has always required privacy. The Swiss Protestant psychiatrist Paul Tournier believes every person needs privacy to become himself, rather than merely a member of a tribe as in totalitarian regimes. A violation of privacy is thus a violation of individuality. The developing child must first assert his individuality, then decide on his own to which intimates he will tell his secrets.

The right to withhold personal information is central to the Fourth and Fifth Amendments to the U.S. Constitution. Many authors concerned about civil liberties have been alarmed in recent years about the loss of privacy via wiretapping, computerized government and credit-agency records, and other forms of surveillance. Professor Arthur R. Miller of the University of Michigan provides a thorough discussion of these new problems against the background of Western legal tradition in *The Assault on Privacy* (1971). Miller takes a dim view of the Freedom of Information Act, because it could be used to invade the privacy of individuals, and is upset over *Life* magazine's victory in a 1967 suit, because it used the First Amendment to limit the right of privacy. Few journalists would go that far, but there has been a growing recognition in the news community that unfair coverage can prejudice trials.

Great Britain puts severe restrictions on its newspapers to prevent influence before or during trials. If Watergate had occurred in London, the press could have printed no investigative reports once the first Republican burglar had been charged. The *Sunday Times* decided to break the law to carry a scorching account on the sufferings of parents whose children had been crippled because the pregnant mothers had taken the drug thalidomide. The press had been prevented from mentioning the tragic situation for ten years while damage suits were tied up in the courts. In the United States there have been some ominous cases of judges binding the press in the name of fair trials. A New York Supreme Court judge barred the press because it reported the alleged underworld ties and criminal record of the defendant, Carmine Persico. An Indiana circuit court judge ejected 13 reporters from a murder trial to prevent prejudicial publicity. In Louisiana a federal district judge fined two reporters for printing testimony heard in open court after he had ordered them not to.

In the Catholic church special factors have reinforced the respect for privacy. Christianity has always recognized a responsibility to the unique, distinct individual. Besides this, counseling, sacramental confession, and penance depend on secrecy. The traditional discussions in moral theology books use the principle of property rights in defending possession of secrets. Information has an "owner" whose rights must be protected. Many texts also treat secrecy under the Eighth Commandment against bearing false witness, because the virtue of veracity is supposedly sinned against by wrongly revealing information, even if it is true. Significantly, the *withholding* of information can also violate the truth commandment, but this is not often discussed.

Moralists also argue from social necessity. It is self-evident that the everyday affairs of individuals and organizations depend on the reliability of secrecy agreements. A friend who breaks confidences soon ceases to be a friend. In this strict sense secrecy is a social good as well as a personal good. The most comprehensive treatment of secrecy among more recent moralists is in Bernard Häring's *The Law of Christ* (1966). He considers secrecy "a stern imperative arising from harsh and evil reality." Since good and evil are at war on earth, indiscretions can cause damage to ourselves, our families, neighbors, or communities. Thus it is forbidden to pry into the secrets of others, to exploit or misuse secrets, or to betray, divulge, or publicize them.

In line with such ethical considerations Western law protects the individual's right of privacy against physical intrusion, use of his name without permission for commercial purposes, publishing of "true but indecent" personal facts, and character assassination. But the U.S. Constitution also guarantees a free press, which may necessitate legitimate invasions of personal privacy. The press argues, with justification, that the person who decides to become a public figure sacrifices his normal right to privacy. In a gray area in between are persons who have public prominence thrust upon them unwillingly, such as relatives of famous persons, or the wives of miners buried in cave-ins. Many persons squirm when a TV reporter thrusts a microphone in front of one of these bereaved victims of fate to pick up a few human-interest comments.

Most moral theologians define three categories of secrets:

Natural secret—To be kept because its revelation would violate justice or charity, under the "laws of nature." Example: publicizing of someone's hidden faults.

Promised secret—To be kept because the recipient promises to protect the information *after* he learns it, as is often done in everyday personal relations.

Entrusted or *committed secret*—To be kept because of an agreement (explicit or implied) *before* the information is disclosed. Often the agreement itself is the reason that the secret is shared.

The most important example of the latter category is the *professional secret* given to a priest, lawyer, or physician in the normal conduct of his services. Journalism does not have the same status as a profession as these other fields, but even so newsmen claim the same sort of secrecy "privilege." They united against the efforts of Attorney General John Mitchell to force them to reveal confidential information. Three such cases were heard eventually by the U.S. Supreme Court, and it decided by a 5 to 4 vote that newsmen must honor subpoenas from grand jury investigations just as other citizens do. The newsmen had contended that, at the least, reporters should not be forced to testify unless there is good reason to believe the reporter has relevant information on crucial matters which is not available from other sources. The importance of the reporter's privilege is that most investigative work depends on confidential sources that will dry up if the sources think the reporter will talk to prosecutors. The Supreme

Court cases involved activities of the Black Panthers and the sale of hashish. (Most reporters who cover the Catholic church would be hamstrung without such confidential sources, but they do not face the complication of investigating possible illicit activity.) The Supreme Court invited Congress to guarantee the newsman's privilege by law if it thought it important, but during the legislative discussions some reporters have opposed the whole idea of making the First Amendment freedom of the press subject to legislation. The dispute extended to TV newsmen when CBS claimed the privilege and refused to provide Congress with the raw material from which it edited a documentary, "The Selling of the Pentagon." During a grand jury probe of the Pentagon Papers leak, Professor Samuel Popkin of Harvard claimed privilege for his confidential sources as a scholar of government and was jailed for a week. Since the Supreme Court ruling a series of newsmen have also served time in prison for refusing to testify.

All three categories of secrets can be broken in certain circumstances, according to the moralists. Typical justifications: The "owner" of the secret gives his consent, or his consent can be presumed; the information is no longer secret, or will definitely become public soon; a lawful authority commands that the information be revealed (though most do not see this as sufficient to break professional secrets); to prevent injustice to an innocent person (again, most exempt professional secrets).

Inquiry into a personal secret is not only permitted, but obligatory under the criteria of justice and love, if this will prevent a greater harm to the community. This justification from the "common good" usually permits even the breaking of the most sacred type, the entrusted secret, because public welfare supersedes individual welfare. But the good to be achieved in breaking the secret must be at least equal to the harm caused to society by relaxing the sanctity of secrets. In other words, there is "common good" to consider on both sides. Traditional moralists make several other exceptions. Parents or boarding-school principals, for example, have been permitted to open children's mail if they have reason to believe a wrong has been committed. Similarly, members of religious orders have often yielded the right of secrecy before their superiors.

In moral theology there is one type of secret which must never be revealed, except with the express permission of the person holding the secret: information which is confessed in the sacrament of Penance. The priest's privilege is so widely recognized that President Nixon cited it in a televised speech explaining why he would not turn tape recordings over to the Watergate grand jury. Catholic annals are replete with stories of martyrs such as St. John Nepomucene who refused to break the "seal" of the confessional. Occasional controversies arise over this in cases of major crimes, since all the states do not recognize the priest's right to silence.

In canon law a priest who violates confessional secrecy is penalized with excommunication. In a bizarre twist the Vatican decreed excommunication for two Italian sociologists who violated confessional secrecy from the other side of the screen. They went through 600 phony "confessions" to priests, mostly on sexual matters, tape recorded the sessions, and made a book out of them.

Traditionally, the confessional stricture has been based theologically on the supernatural character of the sacrament. Some recent writers, however, have been taking the pragmatic approach: without secrecy, the confessional system could never work. Church law provides that a priest need not open his "book of souls" to his bishop, and is exempted from testifying in ecclesiastical trials about matters learned in confidence—even outside the confessional. Does confessional privilege extend beyond the priesthood? In 1971 Sister Margaret Murtha, a New Jersey nun, was jailed when she refused to reveal a confessional-type conversation with a young murder suspect. The experimental liturgy used by the Episcopal Church authorizes a deacon or layman to hear a confession in extraordinary circumstances, and puts him under the priest's secrecy obligation. (For further discussion on Protestant professional confidences see William Tiemann, *The Right to Silence* (1964).

The priestly privilege ran head-on into the interests of the church officialdom during the medieval inquisitions, and the result was very revealing. Heresy was considered heinous, yet unless the confessional seal was guarded the penitent heretic could not give a full, free confession. The solution was to put absolution for heresy outside the powers of the ordinary confessor, so that he was compelled to turn the matter over to his superiors. If a local priest granted absolution for heresy in violation of this rule, there was no safeguard against spiritual "double jeapordy," which would prevent charges of heresy from being lodged against the penitent from higher authorities. If someone incriminated others in his confession, this evidence was not considered sacrosanct either. In fact, some moralists encouraged priests to use the confessional to inquire about heretics. The priests were to write down what was learned, and to transmit the evidence without consent if the penitent did not report it himself. This shows that the interests of the institutional church have at times been considered so crucial as to override even the most sacred category of personal secrecy. So it is predictable that institutional interests would be used to reinforce secrecy in less compelling circumstances.

The Catholic stress upon secrecy in personal relationships doubtless slips over into views on secrecy in social institutions. At first glance, the principles for revealing information to another person would appear to differ only in degree from making such information available to the general public. If secrecy protects individual rights within society, it is a useful counterbalance to the possible abuses of the mass media in our day. The church is well advised to protect its "pastoral" information. An example of this was the tight secrecy surrounding the 1968 Episcopal Church court which heard personal charges against Bishop Joseph Minnis of Denver. The court merely announced that Minnis had violated unspecified ordination vows, and issued an order that he move out of Colorado. From the Catholic standpoint it was noteworthy that the pressure to remove Minnis came from the people of his diocese. A few journalists protested loudly against this closed-door policy, in the name of freedom of the press. But what they were really after was a hot news item. Perhaps reporters in such a case have a professional need to try to unearth what is going on, but the church must first consider its pastoral responsibility to the person involved, unless policy is the matter in dispute.

The Vatican has used the same sort of rationale to apply strict secrecy to hearings involving charges against the orthodoxy or moral character of priests. However, as we have seen, the secrecy has applied not only to the outside world, but to the procedures of the "prosecution," which the "defense" needs to know. Secrecy is also the rule under the present system for nomination of prospects for the office of bishop. All those involved in the process are sworn to consider the process as a "papal secret," which puts it on a level close to that of the confessional seal. Secrecy includes not only the proposal of names, but the F.B.I.-type investigation of candidates to see if there is anything unsavory in their past. If this procedure were public, so the reasoning goes, the negative information, or the fact that a possible candidate was not appointed by the pope, would harm his right to a good reputation. Beyond the regard for individual rights, however, the church is even more concerned that openness would politicize the whole process. There is serious doubt, however, whether this is the best way for the church to choose its leaders. Democratic theory holds that public discussion of potential officials makes it more likely that reasons why a person should not be appointed will come to light before the choice is made, even though there is always a place for confidential evaluations. In the case of bishops this is more crucial because the appointment is for life.

In other words, personal privacy is something to be cherished and defended, but it is not an absolute. The right is easily abused if it is applied thoughtlessly to shield institutions, or to shield the conduct of individual officials within institutions. In these cases the moral principle of the "common good," which is well-established even in the treatment of personal matters, takes hold. The misconduct of an officeholder is dangerous to the community, and common good takes precedence over the person's right to privacy. Secrecy in the institution of the church developed due to historical circumstances, and was nurtured by the pro-secrecy bias in moral theology. Little thought has been given to the "common good" of the community of believers. This failure of theory, as much as anything, explains why the church has been so slow and inconsistent in removing the culture of the cover-up. Catholicism needs to examine—and then apply—the case for candor.

Part III

THE CASE FOR CANDOR

9 To Tell the Truth

Church tradition has vacillated between secrecy and openness, but regardless of what has been done in the past, what *ought* the church to do? If Christian moral and theological principles support freedom of information, they should be applied, regardless of past policies and present convenience. The strong opinion in favor of secrecy in private matters is balanced by a lesser-known Christian rationale in support of candor in the administration of social institutions.

Subsequent chapters will deal with access to information, but the prior consideration is the quality of that information. Any right to information is meaningless if the information is not reliable. Information that is available is all too often misleading, but Christians have a responsibility to contest falsehood wherever it exists. If God is Truth, and Christ is Truth incarnate, truthfulness is the divine standard for all communication.

Contemporary thought has eroded the sound Christian basis for truthtelling. Modern philosophies are not always comfortable with the idea that truth can be conveyed intelligibly through human reason and language. In addition, some modern theologies are not comfortable with the idea of a God who has revealed his personality and his moral will for mankind. And what if the Bible, the most explicit account of this God and of his self-disclosure in Christ, is itself a hopeless admixture of truth and error ranking below what we expect even of the morning newspaper? Yet another theological problem is "situation ethics," under which the command against bearing "false witness" was not etched in stone on Sinai, but is jotted down on the notepad of personal decision (in pencil—in case *agape*-love and circumstances require an erasure). These ideas threaten the validity of all traditional Christian teachings, including the divine command to tell the truth.

Even for traditional-minded theologians, however, "truth" is not simply verbal veracity or a body of accurate information. *Agape* does enter in. Take Rahab, history's most honored prostitute. She is honored in both the Old and New Testaments for lying, lying to protect the lives of two Israelite spies. A much-used modern example is telling a lie to Nazi soldiers to protect the lives of harbored Jews. Truth is communication in a trustworthy, reliable manner within a human relationship.

The great Protestant ethicist Dietrich Bonhoeffer brought similar nuances to the idea of truth. He said a strict definition of truth as thought conforming to speech would rule out both the essential deception of the enemy in wartime as well as the harmless joke. Also the simple discrepancy between speech and thought is an inadequate concept because a deliberate silence can also constitute a lie. (This is a particularly telling point in hierarchical secrecy.) Bonhoeffer also thought that while flattery, hypocrisy, or presumptuous speech might not be materially untrue, they should be considered untruthful because they harm personal relationships. In opposition to Kant, Bonhoeffer sought a moral way to permit conscious lying in Nazi-and-Jew type contexts, but he saw the dangers in situationalism, and his approach should not be confused with the later situation ethics which uses a sentimentalized ethical structure to remove the absolute rule of truthtelling.

Bonhoeffer also knew that "truth" can be used as a weapon. If truth judges persons out of envy and hatred rather than love, it can be "Satanic." Hans Küng thinks that such truth "fanaticism" is a special temptation of Protestantism. He contends that Protestants often exercise "false candor" and carry truthfulness to "ridiculous extremes" by divorcing it from reality. A fanatic "thinks he has the right to say anything at any time to anyone—yes, and even the obligation to do so." The fanatic sets aside responsibility to neighbor and community in his zeal for veracity, even if the specific situation calls for reserve rather than for intrusion. The fanatic believes he has the right to hurt others in the name of honesty, and because he thinks of himself as truthful, he never considers the possibility that he may be wrong. St. Augustine called it *veritas homicida*.

If fanatical truth is the Protestant weakness, fanatical secrecy has sometimes been the Catholic weakness. The reliability of another person's word is certainly as necessary as the sanctity of secrets in preserving that mutual trust upon which the human community depends. Yet the surprising fact is that, in cases of conflict, past Catholic moralists have sometimes considered secrecy to be a higher good than truth itself.

In the past century many Catholic experts have argued in favor of misleading speech in special cases to protect such things as the "common good." Much of this sort of discussion, which has died out recently, involved the sanctity of secret-keeping. In a 1948 treatise Julius Dorszynski argued that a priest may not only practice deceit to protect the confessional seal, but also to hide *any* secret that one ought to keep. Even though he granted a person's "natural right" not to be deceived, he thought that this right should be forfeited to protect a lawful secret from unlawful attempts to obtain it. Therefore, secrets are so important that they justify untruth. (He did add that men entrusted regularly with secrets should learn to speak prudently, and use deception only as a last resort.)

Antony Koch's 1924 morals handbook permitted amphiboly—equivocation, or deliberate use of ambiguous statements with intention to mislead—as a means of evading illicit or even merely curious questions. It was to be used when silence alone would create suspicion.

He argued that in such cases the deception is the listener's fault, since he could decipher the true meaning if he paid closer attention to the exact words. In a 1953 book Francis Connell, then dean of the theology school at Catholic University, offered this "probable" opinion: "When a person is unjustly trying to force me to reveal a truth which I have a right not to reveal, I do not sin if I say something to the contrary. In that event, I am telling a falsehood, but not a lie." He also permitted mental reservation in which a statement *could* be understood in a true sense although, in the actual circumstances, it probably will be understood in another sense. He cautioned that one must have a "good reason for concealing the truth," and that the practice of deception by mental reservation should not be abused. In the light of such games moralists play, reporters interviewing ecclesiastics in those days must have hung skeptically on every word.

Examples the moralists used for allowable deception generally depended upon a higher social good, or protection of personal privacy. For instance: a pupil safeguarding his reputation in front of a classroom; a woman guilty of infidelity and under accusation by her husband; a mother shielding the real reason why her daughter, pregnant out of wedlock, has moved to another city; a soldier captured by the enemy and under interrogation; a priest lying and posing as a truck driver to rescue prisoners; and nonserious instances of social convention ("Mr. Jones is not at home").

The most important recent analysis of this issue among Catholics is that of Bernard Häring. He stated that it was unfortunate that views of mental reservation which had been condemned in the seventeenth century by Pope Innocent XI were revived to distinguish between a morally justifiable falsehood and a lie. In Häring's view the obligation to truthtelling is drawn from God as the source of truth, from the value of one's own uprightness, and from the right of the community to speech which is absolutely trustworthy. Häring does permit exceptions. A secret can be guarded by silence in language or deportment. Since silence or a rebuff can sometimes betray a secret, there may be no course in some situations except to say something which conceals the information. But "even veiled speech must be true." If there is no thought which corresponds to the word, it is a lie, and therefore morally wrong. But evasion is moral if the words can have "multiple meaning" and the purpose is not to deceive, but to protect a truth whose disclosure would violate the law of love of neighbor. The misleading of an "indiscreet inquirer" is permissible if done for a serious reason, if it is the lesser evil, and if deception is not the "necessary result" of the veiled speech.

Beyond such special cases, Catholic moral theology has always supported truthtelling. This includes the church. Häring disparages a quote from Martin Luther that "a good hearty lie for the sake of the good and for the Christian Church, a lie in case of necessity, a useful lie or a serviceable lie, would not be against God." Daniel Callahan's book on *Honesty in the Church* (1965) said that officialdom was guilty of few blatant lies. But he found public dishonesty by the church in other forms: selective presentation of facts; the glossing over of weaknesses; evasiveness; playing upon such sentiments as the members' reverence for the hierarchy. Successful exercise of all of these, except perhaps the last, depends on a shortage of information among the public. Whatever the motives for withholding information, Callahan said, such a practice provides the authorities with "a ready-made excuse to conceal errors, injustices, stupidity, self-seeking, and venality."

Hans Küng, in *Truthfulness* (1968), charged that truth had been made subservient to the institution of the church and the protection of its authority. He said traditional moral theology had shown a "sweeping disregard" for the matter of truth, so much so that it was not even one of the cardinal virtues. "Authority simply determines what is truth, and truth in authoritarianism is what suits authority: its organization, its regime, its system. . . . People adapt themselves. They avoid telling the truth, contradicting authority: 'This is dangerous. It is not true to the party-line, not according to the mind of the

Church.' " This system is justified not out of malice, but "weakness, compliance, desire for peace, tractability, obedience." Unlike the other Catholic theologians of truth, Küng moved directly from personal truthtelling to the issue of open information in the church. He contended that the church must be both truthful and open in order to bear its witness successfully in the world.

Küng and the other moralists have raised notes of caution on the dangerous side of truthtelling in the area of interpersonal communication, rather than the separate matter of transmitting information from an institution to the public. Just as truth is considered a dangerous weapon in personal matters, so the political debates that rage over institutional secrecy raise the dangers to the "security" of the institution that might be created by the revelation of truth. Secrecy can be valuable in personal affairs, as the Catholic tradition insists, and yet be destructive in the conduct of public affairs. Professor Alan Westin put it well in *Privacy and Freedom* (1968): "The democratic society relies on publicity as a control over government, and on privacy as a shield for group and individual life."

10 The Public's Right to Know

When a special committee of the U.S. Senate began investigating the Watergate scandals, the prosecutors feared that the publicly televised hearings would make conviction of the guilty more difficult. Others contended that the public airing of allegations and hearsay would injure the reputations of innocent persons. In the opinion of the much-respected Jesuit weekly *America,* however, such concerns were "exaggerated." The Catholic magazine sided with Chairman Sam Ervin's view that "the public disclosure of this corruption is more important than individual convictions." It said the Senate procedures and a free, competitive press provided built-in correctives to any reckless charges. "There may be some risks in the process of disclosure. But it is the only remedy for the sickness of secrecy now known as Watergate."

In most political situations the release of information carries risks, but so does concealment. Moral theologians and Catholic commentators have recognized that secrecy is sometimes justifiable in the conduct of public business. The issue is at what point the public's right to know should override such considerations as "national security" or "executive privilege." The further issue raised by the present study is the extent to which the case for candor in public institutions can be applied to private organizations in general, and to the church in particular.

109

The typical secular arguments that have been used for and against secrecy were summarized in Chapter 1. A 1969 booklet on the right to know, published by the Council on Religion and International Affairs, is particularly valuable because it bridges the gap between secular politics and moral theology. The main essay was written by William J. Barnds, who had worked in the Office of National Estimates at the Central Intelligence Agency. He said that the citizen's need to know is virtually nonexistent, and the government's need for secrecy high, with such things as diplomatic codes or the technical details of weapons systems. As for diplomacy, Barnds argued that the sensitivities of other, more secretive nations must be taken into account. Foreign officials will not speak openly if they know that what they say will be made public. In addition, he thought secrecy might be necessary in the formation of national policy so that the government could act with a single, coherent voice.

Barnds also discussed the political side of the moral theologians' classic problem of misleading speech for a "good cause." He said that in situations where an official cannot remain silent but must protect secrets, outright lying usually can be avoided. Interestingly, Barnds thought that situationalist Joseph Fletcher was too permissive in inserting "ordinarily" into the Ten Commandments. When the "cover" on intelligence operations was unraveling, Barnds preferred that officials say "no comment." Perhaps in the case of imminent devaluation of currency an outright denial might be essential up to the moment the action is taken. Such are the moral complexities of modern society. The need for secrecy in wartime is readily apparent. Governments deceive the enemy on where they intend to strike in battle, to lower the number of combat deaths. Barnds said that if a government needs to lie, it can probably do so only for a short period, and after that it should generally admit what it did and why. Continual distortion, not the individual lie, is what really damages a society, he concluded.

In comments on the Barnds essay in the C.R.I.A. booklet, Catholic

moralist Daniel Maguire objected to his use of the word "lie," prefer-
ring to talk of the "right to deceive" or the "right to conceal the
truth." And historian Wilson Carey McWilliams commented that
secrecy in wartime is defensible if the public consents to it as necessary. Democracies have had no difficulty in gaining such public support when the need was obvious, and in this way democratic processes
are honored. It should be added that there has been a dangerous trend
in the U.S. which maintains secrecy in diplomacy even *after* an agreement is reached. Even the Congress has been kept in the dark for years
about international agreements made by the executive branch.

McWilliams pointed out that the informing of any mass citizenry
involves a minor form of deception, namely, oversimplification. The
politician or journalist must translate complex political facts into the
everyday idiom. But this simplified translation is justifiable because
without it, many people would lack necessary knowledge. The same
principle obviously applies to the reporting of many theological issues
to a mass audience. Although some bishops raise the same objection
about oversimplification, the procedure is necessary. In fact, it is what
the church practices every week in catechetical instruction and sermons.

Most of the individualistic discussions of secrecy in Catholic moral
theology, surveyed in Chapter 8, include some mention of public
affairs. Moralists traditionally have held that a state secret takes
precedence over a private secret, because of the "common good." Also
because of common good a society has a right to maintain secrets that
are its "property," such as diplomatic and military secrets. The rationale of professional secrets of doctors and others is often carried
over to government officials. Few of the moralists have offered advice
on the criteria for keeping information secret, or on who should apply
the criteria. Moral theology often held that the common good stopped
at the church door. Thus the command of a government official is not
necessarily sufficient to free a priest from his obligation to keep secrets, even secrets learned *outside* the confessional. A 1941 treatise

argued that in such cases the priest is justified in using mental reservation and may "reply that he does not know; even, if necessary, taking an oath to that effect." On the other hand, the secret may be revealed if the command is "just" and no "grave scandal" results.

In public affairs, under what conditions should secrets be broken? As we have seen, the moralists state that justice and love may require that private good be subordinated to the public good. In his 1924 handbook Koch said secrecy should not be used to cover up dishonest dealings, create false opinions, spread lying reports, or do anything to injure public confidence. Spying and wiretapping, which violate privacy, often have been justified if they are used to prevent a great evil, but moral theology has considered them a last resort.

Modern Christian theologians who have dealt with the ethics of public affairs have largely ignored the question of secrecy. One of the strongest arguments against secrecy came from Karl Barth, the century's leading Protestant theologian. He did not base his case upon democratic theory, but upon the nature of God:

> The Church lives from the disclosure of the true God and His revelation, from Him as the Light that has been lit in Jesus Christ to destroy the works of darkness. It lives in the dawning of the day of the Lord and its task in relation to the world is to rouse it and tell it that this day has dawned. The inevitable political corollary of this is that the Church is the sworn enemy of all secret policies and secret diplomacy. It is just as true of the political sphere as of any other that only evil can want to be kept secret. The distinguishing mark of the good is that it presses forward to the light of day. Where freedom and responsibility in the service of the State are one, whatever is said and done must be said and done before the ears and eyes of all, and the legislator, the ruler, and the judge can and must be ready to answer openly for all their actions—without thereby being necessarily dependent on the public or allowing themselves to be flurried. The state-craft that wraps itself up in darkness is the craft of a state which, because it is anarchic or tyrannical, is forced to hide the bad conscience of its citizens or officials. The Church will not on any account lend its support to that kind of State.

By contrast, Catholic writers on public affairs often came out on the side of secrecy, especially at the height of the Cold War. One important issue was President Truman's Executive Order 10290, which for the first time extended the military system of classified documents to the civilian agencies. Under the order, any department could decide on its own to withhold any information if it thought secrecy served the national interest. In his first year in office President Eisenhower, himself a former general, revised the Truman plan with a new executive order that has been followed with only minor changes ever since. It is important to realize that the neither system of "classified" documents was never enacted into law by the Congress. Even the dean of a Catholic journalism school, J. L. O'Sullivan of Marquette University, stressed national security to the near-exclusion of the value of free information in an article on the Truman order. O'Sullivan was skeptical about the press, which is the major channel of public information, because he thought it was less immediately responsible to the public than most government officials were.

An editorial in the Passionist Fathers' *The Sign* in 1949, concerning a United Nations discussion of freedom of information, complained that Americans have a "boundless faith in the integrity of the press." The magazine thought that American delegates to the U.N. had argued for too little restriction on publishing, a stand as misguided as the Soviet Union's campaign for a controlled press, because "the press is entitled to no such exaggerated confidence." For instance, it had given a distorted picture of the Spanish Civil War. Incredibly, the editorial concluded: "We see little to choose between the personal dictatorship of a politician and the institutional dictatorship of the press."

Fortunately, such opinions have not been typical. John O'Brien was able to use the pages of *The Sign* in 1952 to criticize the Truman executive order. He said the press has the primary duty to restrict censorship in government and to dig out information, and that the public should help by pressuring Congress to guarantee access to information. This idea finally achieved some success in 1966, with the

Freedom of Information Act, although the act has had virtually no impact on the mountain of documents rated as "classified" by the executive branch. L. J. Beaufort, who was a priestly delegate to the U.N. discussion of secrecy, contended that the Soviet concept of press control was based on the supposed good of the people collectively, to the exclusion of the good of individuals. (This is another possible outcome, then, of the moralists' "common good.") Beaufort termed freedom of information "an individual right, connected with an individual responsibility," which, however, should not be used to endanger peace, security, or the rights recognized by the U.N.

The Jesuit weekly *America* has consistently defended access to information. As far back as 1932 an editorial worried about the suppression of facts which was ordered to try to crack the Lindbergh kidnaping case. The magazine criticized the view commonly held by Europeans and moral theologians that the public has no right to know what is happening if the knowledge is harmful to the common good. *America* said that the U.S. has always believed that "most often this procedure allows crooked politicians to rob the public with impunity, or blundering statesmen to plunge the State into unnecessary war. . . . There is little doubt in the United States that the utmost publicity in the people's own affairs consonant with the public safety is the surest safeguard of liberty in a democracy." The magazine, however, recognized no public right to information about the purely domestic affairs of prominent men, since mere curiosity has no rights. And *America* feared that unless the press practiced restraint in such matters it might invite government censorship. Discussing the Truman executive order in 1953, *America* stated that the more government affects our lives "the more obnoxious its secret operations become. We have learned to distrust official conduct shielded from public knowledge." The editorial granted that secrecy in diplomatic and military matters can be in the national interest, but—unlike most moral theologians in those days—*America* wondered about who would make the decisions. It is dangerous to let public officials decide these questions at will, the magazine believed, because they are interested parties. Three years later an essayist in the magazine proposed an appeals board to settle disputes about the public right to inspect documents.

During the years since World War II when information debates have become so important, the Papacy has taken a particular interest in freedom of information. The pioneer in this new emphasis was Pope Pius XII, who was the grandson of the co-founder of *L'Osservatore Romano*, Marcantonio Pacelli. Pius issued dozens of statements on mass communications. He regarded the press as the essential source of information for most people, and praised its essential service to society. His successor, Pope John XXIII, who had an early ambition to be a journalist, provided a major papal recognition of the right to information. His encyclical *Pacem in Terris* (1963) described rights of man which carry "authoritative force" under natural law and are "universal and inviolable, and therefore altogether inalienable." John stated that each person has dignity under divine revelation because men, through God's grace, "have been ransomed by the blood of Jesus Christ." After laying this strong foundation, John listed this right:

> Man has a right to freedom in investigating the truth, and—within the limits of the moral order and the common good—to freedom of speech and publication, and the freedom to pursue whatever profession he may choose. He has the right, also, to be accurately informed about public events.

Pope Paul VI's father was the longtime editor of a small provincial daily, and as Monsignor Montini, Paul wrote the constitution for the International Union of Catholic Press in the 1930s. In an October 1963 speech to the union Pope Paul repeated Pope John's assertion that the right to information is part of man's very nature, then added:

> . . . it evidently does not suffice to proclaim it in theory; one must also recognize this right in practice, defend it, serve it, and so direct its exercise that it remains faithful to its natural purpose. The right is at once active and passive: the seeking of information, and the possibility for all to receive it.

The many statements of Pius, John, and Paul have articulated a theology of social information. A summary of the major points:

The press is no substitute for preaching, the primary apostolate, since it describes events as they are in fact, and reflects the nonsacred character of human life. Even the Catholic press is basically "profane" in this sense. But the press has a "sacred" task when it leads the reader to spiritual truth. The church cannot be aloof from the press, because it spreads church teaching on both temporal and spiritual questions. Information is essential in modern society, because it enables the citizen to understand situations and to make responsible decisions. Access to information is justified, because it improves individuals and the community, but to do this the information must be ethical, sensitive to the nature of man, true, factual, and objective. Sin and untruth can be caused by omission as well as by commission, so no one has the right to publish only what agrees with his own opinions and ignore other information. Information should not be degraded into propaganda, appeal to man's passions, or arouse one group against another. Information must stop short of harming a person's right to good reputation and to legitimate secrecy in his private life. Not all information is good for all people—youth in particular should be protected —so the common good must be respected. Despite the need for objectivity, news should go beyond the superficial; the expression of thought beyond the mere recitation of facts is legitimate. The press should affect public opinion rather than just being molded *by* it. To operate effectively the press must have freedom (not license) of thought and expression, limited by the demands of the common good, and of truth.

This body of papal teaching was paralleled in Vatican Council II's *Decree on the Media of Social Communication,* which Paul promulgated on December 4, 1963. The key passage on information reads:

> Therefore, in society men have a right to information, in accord with the
> circumstances in each case, about matters concerning individuals or the

community. The proper exercise of this right demands, however, that the news itself that is communicated should always be true and complete, within the bounds of justice and charity. In addition, the manner in which the news is communicated should be proper and decent. This means that in both the search for news and in reporting it, there must be full respect for the laws of morality and for the legitimate rights and dignity of the individual. For not all knowledge is helpful, but "it is charity that edifies."

Although the decree was historic in providing recognition of the media by an ecumenical council, it has been roundly criticized by both journalists and ecclesiastics. Monsignor Vincent Yzermans commented that the history of the decree "has been considered by most American conciliar participants and observers as something just a little short of tragedy." Among other things, the critics said the decree imposed churchly demands upon Catholics working in the media which are nearly impossible for them to follow if they want to remain professionals. In the *New Catholic Encyclopedia* Catholic journalist John Deedy said that the recognition of the right to information was so hedged that "information could become less a right of the uninformed person or the communicator than a discretion to be exercised in whole, or part, or not at all, by the person who is the source of the information." The decree protected reserve on the part of authorities without pointing out that this is an impediment to the basic right to information.

The U.S. Bishops' Committee for Social Communications issued a more satisfactory statement on the right to information in 1967. And in 1973 the Communication Committee of the U.S. Catholic Conference, with the approval of the bishops' administrative board, released a warning about the importance of press freedom which specified the responsibilities of officials:

Public authorities must also play a positive role in insuring the free flow of information by making information readily available to the public through the news media. This does not mean that public officials must disclose everything they know about every subject; in some cases this might do more harm than good. But it is equally true that public officials have a duty to explain their policies and actions to the people and, in doing so, to provide information which is "full, consistent, accurate and true." Where decisions must be made whether to disclose or withhold information, the general presumption should be in favor of disclosure.

Although the papal statements and the Vatican II decree were explicit about the obligations of the secular and church media to the church, they said nothing of the obligations of the church to the media. Nor did they discuss the crucial matter of whether the right to information applies within the church itself. The closest the council decree came to this was a paragraph on the need for the Catholic press to form church public opinion and "disseminate and properly explain news concerning the life of the church." For the media covering the church, Deedy said, Vatican II offered no guarantee that the condition had progressed from the state of "prying news from those reluctant about imparting any information except that which reflects advantageously on the sources' concern." If freedom of information within the church was not specified by the council fathers, neither was it excluded from the general statements about the right to information.

The church is not alone in neglecting this issue, since relatively little has been written by secular theorists about freedom of information in nonpublic organizations, either in their internal affairs or in their responsibilities to the society at large. The private group is most obviously accountable where it intersects with public affairs, and with legitimate public interest. A good deal of this is common-sense cooperation. When the church constructs a major school or hospital, the secular government must be involved in planning traffic access and utility services. Sometimes the internal policies of a private organization are of such significance to the wider society that the public has a right to this information. James Russell Wiggins in *Freedom or Secrecy* (1964) used the example of a local church which decided to integrate racially but wanted to avoid publicity to prevent trouble. Wiggins argued that the policy change was important enough to society that the public had a right to know about it. Private organizations that are strongly opposed to the "common good," such as organized crime, radical revolutionaries, or the Ku Klux Klan, may require special scrutiny on the part of the broader society, although Christians differ on the extent and methods of surveillance which are ethically justifiable.

The clearest ties of private organizations to the society are financial. Private corporations obviously affect the public sphere directly; they stand to lose public confidence—and business—if they practice total secrecy. Religious and other nonprofit groups benefit from tax exemption and other direct public benefits, and the society must determine whether these privileges are legitimate. Certainly their books should be open at least to officials, and the 1969 federal tax reform act requires nonprofit, tax-exempt groups to file income statements that are open to public inspection. This law, however, exempts the agencies of a church body from filing.

Wiggins, who believes in the accountability of private organizations to the general public, says that this duty is increasingly recognized, not so much in law as in the *de facto* assertion of rights by the public and by members of private organizations. Strictly speaking, he admits, a private group is fully accountable only to its members. But "the public's right to know seems on solid ground where the organization involved is a quasi-public agency, even though it has only an informal or social connection with public institutions."

Alan F. Westin of Columbia University is so concerned with the erosion of the right to individual privacy that he argues for a considerable right to secrecy for private groups. In *Privacy and Freedom* (1968) he contended that all organizations, including government agencies, need the right to decide when, and to what extent, their actions should be made public. In democracies the decision is weighted in favor of "earlier disclosure and greater visibility." The loss of secrets, for instance diplomatic or trade information, can threaten the independence of an organization. Controversial groups may need secret membership lists to avoid social pressure against members, which could cause defections and destroy the organization. Catholics have protected such information not only under antiChristian governments, but under Protestant persecution. And some fearful Protestant congregations in Spain, mindful of past persecution, have refused to register under the "freedom of religion" law partly because it requires them to file membership lists. Secrecy to protect institutional survival or to prevent oppression of members of a private group is certainly justifiable. Westin, however, would deny the right of privacy to such "illegitimate" organizations as the K.K.K.

Westin thinks the government should not interfere with the internal policy and discipline of private groups, because they need privacy to keep up a "public face" and maintain "the gap between public myth and organizational reality." He cites churches as an example. Society has an image of how churches ought to operate, including rational decision-making and fair-minded discussion. However, the church should consider truth more important than "image." Westin also says that members of voluntary organizations must be able to relax, communicate freely with one another, and accomplish their tasks with a minimum of "social dissembling for 'outside' purposes," which could "seriously impair" the operations of the group. Union elections, corporation finances, and regulatory commission hearings are "so charged with public interest" that Westin agrees they should be open.

Westin mingles consideration of public bodies with private organizations, implying that there are no essential differences between them. If so, a private organization has not only the right to preserve itself, but some sort of accountability to *its own membership,* a question that Westin ignores. It also has obligations to the general public, which even this privacy-oriented author admits. In matters that affect the general public, Westin is mainly concerned about preserving technical secrets (trade data) or shielding preliminary consideration of matters which will later become public. Another major weakness of his discussion is that there are many kinds of private organizations, with different levels of public accountability. The Catholic church, with 48 million baptized members in the U.S., has different responsibilities from a small-town club with two dozen members.

Discussion of private organizations should also distinguish the diffferent kinds of information that might be at issue. In the example of the church, the communication of three types of *content* is implicit in the above chapters:

1. The *sacred*—Doctrine, ethical teaching, Scripture, liturgy, the miraculous, and other spiritual matters. Psychiatrist Paul Tournier wrote that "secrecy makes things valuable. . . . Every church has rites whose meanings have the prestige of secrecy." Strictly speaking, the general public has a minimal right to know about such things, but Catholics today believe that most sacred matters should be made public—indeed are commanded by God to be made public. There is less agreement on how to treat speculative and investigative work by Catholic theologians.

2. The *pastoral* and *personal*—As we have seen, the church's regard for persons, and its whole system of counseling and confession, have emphasized the benefits of privacy in these areas.

3. The *administrative*—This is the arena of current change and controversy, and in which Catholicism is in the process of trading the style of recent centuries for an earlier style of openness. Though patterns of administrative information may be entrenched, they are not immutable aspects of divine revelation.

Another way to categorize information is by three types of *relation* between the church officialdom and the public:

1. *Purely internal church matters*—For instance, changes in the liturgy. Here it could be argued that the church is accountable only to its own membership, but also that church officials must provide full information to the church-owned press. Bishops should be particularly accountable to their own people, but in practice they cannot

reveal much to them without making it open to the general public—at least in the American situation. Besides this, the Catholic community has become dependent upon independent church publications and the secular media, so the realities of the situation necessitate cooperation with nonofficial media to inform the Catholic public.

2. *Internal church matters with public consequences*—For instance, church teaching on birth control. The stand against artificial contraception is of dramatic social significance in an age of population pressures. And it has become a political issue in places such as Ireland, where the church-inspired ban on contraception in the southern Republic is one of the many reasons the Protestant majority of Northern Ireland resists unification. Since God has placed men in society and has placed Catholics in society with non-Catholics, contraception and many other matters of church teaching cannot be considered to be purely internal, since they directly affect nonmembers. Thus the outsiders have as legitimate a right to be informed on these matters as they do of information on secular government.

3. *Church influence on purely secular matters*—The American bishops usually seek, and receive, wide publicity when they make a declaration on a social issue. In their lobbying activity, such as for parochial school aid, they are less noticed, and less interested in being noticed. But when the church inserts itself into a secular, external issue, it assumes the same responsibilities for information that are expected of secular groups. This is particularly true if the church seeks financial or other benefits from the public. Vatican II recognized that such public desire for information is legitimate, and if the public cannot get it, its regard for the church suffers accordingly.

Catholic moral theology has provided little discussion on the question of the public accountability of private organizations in general. There is one major exception, however: the extensive material on the polemical issue of "secret societies" such as the Masons. This lodge has been intertwined with Catholic history in Europe and the U.S. Papal bulls in 1738, 1751, 1821, and 1825 condemned membership in such groups under pain of excommunication. The major factor in the papal condemnations was the opinion that various organizations were opposed to both church and state. But secrecy was also a factor. Canon law indicates that the problem was not secrecy *per se,* but secrecy which was maintained in the face of rightful inquiries of church and state authorities. Harmless lodge secrets for the purpose of amusement or sustaining the interest of members, such as those used by the Catholic Knights of Columbus, were not forbidden, so long as they were enforced merely by a "gentlemen's agreement," rather than an oath before God. Several Protestant groups, notably the Lutheran Church—Missouri Synod, agree with Catholicism on this issue.

When the U.S. bishops assembled in Baltimore in 1843, they issued a pastoral letter which warned against joining any organization "the objects of which are not distinctly declared," and where oaths or similar arrangements are used "to veil the ends of the association, or its proceedings, from the public eye. . . . Since all just objects may be openly avowed and pursued, the mantle of secrecy is needlessly thrown around them." At the bishops' Baltimore meeting of 1884 a lengthy section of the pastoral letter was again devoted to secret societies. It said:

> There is one characteristic which is always a strong presumption against a society, and that is secrecy. Our Divine Lord Himself has laid down the rule: "Every one that doth evil hateth the light and cometh not to the light, that his works may not be reproved. But he that doth truth cometh to the light that his works may be made manifest, because they are done in God." When, therefore, associations veil themselves in secrecy and darkness, the presumption is against them, and it rests with them to prove that there is nothing evil in them.

It is significant that beyond any evidence of evil practices, the American bishops considered secrecy as an evil in itself, a separate criterion for the Christian to use in deciding whether an organization was legitimate and in harmony with the Christian life. The bishops, however, also recognized that justice may require secrecy in special circumstances. The most important instance in America was the Knights of Labor, a pioneer union. The U.S. hierarchy interceded successfully with the Vatican to prevent condemnation of the Knights, on the grounds that secrecy was needed to protect it from very real enemies, and that full information was provided to authorities.

So the Catholic church has a well-established teaching against secrecy, not only in public institutions, but in private organizations. The U.S. bishops have said that secrecy by itself is a presumption against an organization. On the basis of the church's own standard, the public has had reason in the past to distrust Catholicism. Should Catholicism be true to its teachings in its own internal conduct? Or is the church theologically exempt from the standards that it has established for other organizations?

11 Is the Church Exempt?

Christians do not think of the church as just another private organization. Unlike I.T.T., the United Auto Workers, or the Society for the Preservation and Encouragement of Barber Shop Quartet Singing in America, it is supernatural as well as natural in character. What the church teaches about freedom of information elsewhere might not apply automatically at home. There are several avenues that can be followed in making this application, including the new view of the church since Vatican II, the natural law view of man and other theological tenets, and various church statements that culminated in the first high-level recognition of freedom of information in the church in 1971.

Traditional Catholic ecclesiology has emphasized the church's supernatural aspect, tending to describe it in the abstract as a static entity. It has also asserted the superiority of the church over secular society. In society authority comes from below; in the church it comes from above. But since Vatican II Catholic scholars have balanced the sublime, supernatural interpretation of the church with new emphasis on past sins of the popes and the people of God. And they have reemphasized the historical and conditional aspect of the church by describing how it has changed in different times and places. Indeed, the church is aware that its status has changed radically in recent years in so-called "Catholic countries."

125

It is evident that the church's interpretation of itself does shift in relation to temporal influences. In *The Church Among the People* (1969) Irish journalist John Horgan showed how social conditions in different countries have produced varying styles of Catholicism. As John McKenzie commented, "the Church in the course of its history has reflected the features of the absolute monarchical state, the feudal state, the army, and, in modern times, the corporation. Although the Church has yet to reflect the features of the democratic or the republican state, there is no reason to think that it will not."

Many liberal Catholic writers on ecclesiology have written about the "democratic church," an unpopular idea with most bishops and traditionalists. Although freedom of information is honored in secular democracies, the church need not become a democracy also in order to grant this freedom. In the rhetoric of antidemocratic Catholics the main concern is that religious doctrine not be sacrificed to the whims of popular sentiment, as though eternal truth could be determined by Gallup polls. On this point a distinction has been drawn by William Willoughby, a conservative Protestant who writes a breezy column on religion in the Washington *Evening Star-News.* In a piece on Catholic secrecy he said that the church "will be weak if it ends up as a democracy. In matters of doctrine, it was never intended that the will of the majority should be what determines the way men should believe." On the other hand, "in non-doctrinal matters, right from the start, it was the people who had the say."

The church need not become a full-fledged democracy in order to take its teaching about information in the secular state and apply it to itself. But there should be good theological grounds for the application. In studying the mysterious interplay between the human and the divine, on information or any other issue, the classical Protestant approach is to proceed from God to man. For instance, Karl Barth began his treatment of political secrecy with God's self-revelation, and concluded that the open society was an essential application of the divine will. The important 1971 Pastoral Instruction from the papal communications commission followed a similar motif. It stated that when man turned away from God, human discord and lack of communication resulted. But God again initiated communication with man. At the climax of this salvation history "he communicated his very self to man and 'the Word was made flesh.' " The life, death, and resurrection of Jesus Christ communicated God's truth with all men more richly than ever before. Jesus also laid the foundation for communication among men, because God had provided the supreme example of communication by himself becoming man. Jesus ordered the disciples continually to spread the Good News "in the light of day" and "from the rooftops." In his ministry on earth Christ revealed himself as the "Perfect Communicator," preaching the divine message without compromise while adjusting to the speech and thought of his culture. In the Eucharist Christ established the most perfect, intimate form of continuing communication between God and man.

In traditional Thomism theological analogy is used as the link between the human and the divine. Thomas Aquinas recognized the existence of a gap between the Creator and the created so vast that the very possibility of knowledge of God depends upon analogies. Since human knowledge proceeds from sense data interpreted by reason, the link of analogy is essential for all knowledge of the nature of a God who is spiritual, infinite, and thus beyond man's sensual and rational comprehension. This is true even of revealed knowledge of God, since God cannot reveal his mysteries to man except through concepts which are intelligible to the human mind. Through the elements of perfection which exist within all finite beings, we can gain a knowledge of the attributes of infinite Being. Sensible things are effects of God, and every effect of God is in some way analagous to its Cause. In this way traditional Catholic thought proceeds from the natural to the supernatural.

In Catholic theology natural law is part of the system which emanates from the reason of God. It is the transcendent, unchanging reflection of divine reason inherent in all things created by God. In scholastic philosophy natural law has an ontological aspect, referring to its nature apart from material existence, and a gnosiological aspect, in its capacity to be known through man's practical reason. The underlying principles in all things remain the same through changing circumstances, but the application of these principles in human law can vary endlessly.

According to Catholic philosophy, there is such a thing as human nature, and the rights and responsibilities of man have a rational foundation. Medieval Catholic theology stressed the responsibilities; philosophy since the eighteenth century has stressed the rights. Jacques Maritain and other modern Catholic philosophers have turned to natural law to seek the basis of such elemental human rights as man's economic, social, individual, moral, and spiritual freedoms. In each of these, knowledge (and information) is an implicit component.

Thomas believed in the superiority of church over state, because it reflects a higher authority. But if man's rights are based on natural law, there can be no conflict between them and divine law (i.e., God's revelation, as in the Bible). Analogy suggests, therefore, that man's moral and spiritual freedom is to operate in church as well as in state. In view of Catholicism's administrative development along authoritarian lines, it is interesting to note that Thomas himself stressed the free moral agency of man—even in the ultimate matters of religious truth. He taught that a ruler must not limit the moral autonomy of his subjects, and that where one did so, resistance of this tyranny was not only permissible, but a duty. Thomas was against forced conversions, and did not think the church should punish unbelief in those who had never received Christianity, though he regarded apostasy from the faith as another matter.

Thomism placed greater esteem on man's potential than did such Protestant theological strands as Calvinism. Man's reason was of course finite, but his perception was not permanently darkened by the Fall. This high view of the individual man, and of his rights, assumes the availability of knowledge to foster his growth as a fully mature Christian.

The natural law would not apply to the church if divine revelation took precedence over the naturally derived principle and excluded institutional self-disclosure in the church. But in this research no such secrecy principle was discovered in revelation. One of the best applications of the natural law tradition directly to the issue of information has been written by Emile Gabel, an Augustinian who was formerly editor of the French Catholic daily *La Croix,* and then director of the International Union of Catholic Press. Writing for *America* in 1963, he argued that man's natural right to information has usually been bluntly denied in the church, due to the hierarchical nature of its government, and a tradition where "in many spheres a policy of secrecy has won hands down." But any natural right is universal, inviolable, and inalienable, and must be respected in any society. The church, especially since it is the guardian of natural law, should not deprive a layman of a right which "he possesses by reason of his dignity as a human person, that is, a right rooted in the very substance of his being." Church members have a right to "objective, ample, and permanent information" not *even* in the church, but most especially and to a heightened degree in the church. Every government sometimes needs to use silence to increase its "efficiency, justice, and prudence," yet all governments tend to expand these "zones of silence." Since the church is partly historical, its members bring to church life the "needs and exigencies" to which they are accustomed in secular society. Thus church structures and customs must necessarily be open to change, Gabel argued. The church is not just a hierarchy in modern theology, but a community. If not democratic in structure, "it can and must be democratic in practice." Although the church is a divine institution as well as a human one, "adoration does not exclude the right to know."

A Catholic social doctrine that applies to secrecy is subsidiarity. The concept was first stated in Pope Leo XIII's social encyclical

Rerum Novarum (1891), and was developed in Pope Pius XI's *Quadragesimo Anno* (1931) and Pope John XXIII's *Mater et Magistra* (1961). Subsidiarity means that it is an evil disruption of the proper social order to transfer to a larger, higher administrative level any function which can be performed at a lower level. Decentralization of function also means decentralization of power and responsibility, and this is impossible without the dissemination of full, reliable information. So if the church is subject to its own social teaching, it must apply subsidiarity in its information processes.

A more recent but well-established idea in Catholic theory is co-responsibility in the life of the church. The Advisory Council, which represents various elements of the U.S. church in discussions with the bishops, described it this way: "The basic idea of the Church in Vatican II is that of a people, a communion, a fellowship in which all are called to the dignity and freedom of the sons of God, thanks to the Holy Spirit who dwells in all members." Implicit in such shared responsibility is the sort of accountability to the membership that is taken for granted in Catholic expectations of secular leaders.

Martin H. Work, one of America's outstanding Catholic laymen, relates this directly to information. Work himself has been active in the practice of co-responsibility. When Pope Paul decided to add laymen to the official observers at Vatican II, Work, then the executive director of the National Council of Catholic Men, was one of three Americans he appointed. Since then Work has become a pioneering modern-day *oeconomus,* as the director of administration and planning for the Archdiocese of Denver. Work is also one of the 15 members of Pope Paul's international advisory council of laymen. Work believes that information will help the people of God become intelligently co-responsible in a church which is a community, rather than a corporation or a bureaucracy. And he thinks information is an "extremely important" moral issue for the church:

> The Church is a mystery in a theological sense, but not a mystery in a secular sense—at least it shouldn't be. Its basic stance should be one of

openness, honesty, and charity in dealing not only with the individual, but
with all of the members of the Church. Those in authority hold accountability to the membership as well as accountability to God. So I am for free,
open flow of information in the Church and to the public.

However, Work does not believe that everyone must know everything. He proposes a "need to know" principle—if "need" is defined
very broadly. The greater the person's responsibility in the church, the
greater the need. A member of a diocesan pastoral council must know
a great deal about church administration, but not a Christmas-and-
Easter Catholic. Work thinks the church should define principles to
govern the release of information, to be developed at all levels by
leaders and representatives of the membership. "I would decide the
question on the basis of whether there was greater good to come to
the Church by revealing matters or by keeping them secret. Of course,
my concept of what the good of the Church is might not coincide with
that of a lot of other people." Along similar lines, Michael Kennedy
wrote in *U.S. Catholic* that a bishop, like any leader, must be able to
keep his future options open, and this requires some secret planning.
But Kennedy said canon law should define what information the
members have a right to know and in what areas leaders should be
permitted to exercise a right to secrecy.

There is little ethical discussion in print in support of secrecy
policies. Officials have made use of the concept of "scandal," defined
in moral theology as a word or action which causes another person's
spiritual ruin. With the traditional, idealized view of the Catholic
church as the only channel of salvation on earth, information which
would harm the people's image of the church or its leaders supposedly
would cause "scandal." Francis X. Murphy, the well-known American moral theologian, says scandal is translated as "not setting a bad
example, not giving the shock treatment, and not upsetting the Catholic faith. Ninety per cent of the sins committed in the name of secrecy
are justified by saying, 'We don't want to give scandal to the people.'

What does this mean? What will the reaction of the people really be? The justification has no foundation in fact."

What about Westin's rationale for secrecy in private organizations, outlined in the preceding chapter? There are relatively few internal matters which directly affect the ongoing *survival* of the church as an institution. Where survival is truly at stake, as it may well be under some current totalitarian regimes, the Christian community may be forced to surrender its normative lifestyle and operate secretly. Such emergency conditions exist for Christian groups in many Communist lands, where the regimes have used information on finances and membership to persecute the church. Even in these cases the obligations of leaders to inform members should be met as fully as possible. In such risky situations Christians and journalists elsewhere may be required to withhold information the release of which would be damaging to these oppressed churches.

As for Westin's worry about the harm to the church "image" through openness, this is a singularly sub-Christian approach for deciding what ought to be done. In any case, John McKenzie balances this by pointing out the harm that secrecy also causes to the church's image. "The public somewhat stubbornly adheres to its belief that no one hides things except those who have something to hide. The public sees no motive for the secrecy which envelops so much of ecclesiastical administration except the fear that the administration would be ashamed of some things if the secrecy were lifted." He says that the image of authority is much less tarnished by public discussion of church issues than it is by secret policy-making, which can debase authority by mixing prejudice, gossip, and irrelevancies into policy-making which would never have survived in mature, public deliberation.

Whatever the justifications for secrecy, Catholic authorities in recent times have begun to be more interested in the values of openness. The evolution of teaching began at the papal level with recognition of the importance of public opinion within the church. In a very significant statement in February 1950 Pope Pius XII said that the church is "a living body, and something would be lacking in its life were public opinion to be missing in it, a deficiency for which both pastors and the faithful would be to blame." Although Pius did not say so, his recognition of church public opinion implied recognition of the need for information, which is essential to public opinion. In *Free Speech in the Church* (1959), Karl Rahner cautioned that Pius' statement had no doctrinal authority, and was not even published in the official Vatican acts. Yet Rahner wrote in 1959—before Vatican II made it official—that the church would have to specify the need for church public opinion. Rahner included morals, liturgy, and administration, but not dogma, under public opinion, and said on these "any form of 'top secret' government would be a really great danger."

In a 1966 letter to a sociology seminar in France the then Vatican Secretary of State, Cardinal Cicognani, said church public opinion existed "in matters open to free discussion," and that it corresponded to Vatican II's new emphasis upon the laity as the people of God rather than as mere subjects. "It is therefore normal and healthy that a public opinion should develop among the faithful and express itself freely. For the Church lives and develops in history" and public opinion in the church is a "manifestation of the holy liberty of the children of God." The late Richard Cardinal Cushing of Boston issued a pastoral letter on public opinion in 1963 which said one element in it is "reaction to abuses which, through human frailty, may at any time be developing within the Church as an institution. . . . The more mature the society and the more committed its members become to the implications of their faith, the more sure are we to have a living ferment of Christian thought among us."

The authoritative recognition of this new emphasis in ecclesiology came in Vatican II's *Dogmatic Constitution on the Church:*

An individual layman, by reason of the knowledge, competence, or outstanding ability which he may enjoy, is permitted and sometimes obliged to express his opinion on things which concern the good of the Church. When occasions arise, let this be done through the agencies set up by the Church for this purpose. Let it always be done in truth, in courage, and in prudence, with reverence and charity toward those who by reason of their sacred office represent the person of Christ.

This guarded wording shows that the council did not consider the church to be a democracy, but that it should have democratic elements in its life. Despite the obvious relation of freedom of information to public opinion, the council did not make the connection between the two.

Liberal Catholic scholars took the next step, extending the public opinion principle to candor and openness in church life. Hans Küng said that postconciliar application of decrees could hardly be carried out properly by groups whose membership is secret and which "meet away from the light of publicity." He praised the Dutch Pastoral Councils, where all levels in the church and even outside observers "deliberate and make decisions freely and openly." He said the reform of canon law is inconceivable without the widest possible discussion and consultation. Such work cannot be dominated by an administrative body such as the Vatican Curia, "nor may it take place in secret; it must be accounted for publicly in the Church." He also said policy-making and budget-making are inevitably connected. "Open budgeting and presentation of accounts of the use of church monies in parish, the nation, and the Church as a whole is essential." Similarly, Küng wrote in *Why Priests?* (1972) that "there must be sufficient transparency to assure all members of the Church, at least potentially, a look into the important activities of the Church and its leadership. To this belongs not least—since financial and pastoral decisions are often closely linked—open budgeting and accountability for the use of Church funds at the local, regional and world-wide levels. On all important questions, information and communication must flow, not only from 'above' to 'below,' but also back from 'below' to 'above.' " Though Küng asserts strongly the right to information, he does not provide any substantial argumentation. In fact, this is a task that few Catholic reformers have attempted, just as the practitioners of secrecy have failed largely to provide any justification for their policies. Perhaps secrecy grew up without a rational basis and must be attacked on other than rational terms.

At the time when the U.S. Congress was debating the Freedom of Information Act, Hugh Morley, the United Nations representative of the Catholic press union, wrote an article which applied the secular discussion to the church. The fact that perfect, infallible, and objective information is a human impossibility, he said, is no excuse for halting information. "Even imperfect transmittal of truth is preferable to withholding it. And open dialogue on a controversial, 'dangerous' truth is preferable to secrecy." Since laymen share access to the sources of grace with the clergy, he reasoned, they should enjoy a free flow of communication with the clergy.

Finally, the new concept of the right to information has been gaining explicit recognition among the hierarchy, and has become a part of the teaching of the Catholic church. One of the firmest statements was in the celebrated interview with Leo Josef Cardinal Suenens of Belgium, which appeared in 1969 in the *Informations Catholiques Internationales* of Paris:

> I am convinced that there is a great liberating force in the honest expression of what one profoundly believes to be true. "The truth," said Jesus, "will make you free." Truth can best be seen in the open air. I know that it may seem more diplomatic to deal with problems behind closed doors, but though I do appreciate the value of secret diplomacy in some cases, I do not believe in secrecy over pastoral matters, and secrecy in itself serves only to maintain the *status quo*.

Fully a dozen years before Suenens said that, the entire American hierarchy recognized the right to information when it issued a pastoral letter on censorship. The bishops said freedom of the press is bound up with "man's right to knowledge," and that "the right to know the truth is evidently broad and sweeping." In 1967 the U.S. Bishops' Communications Committee issued a statement which applied the teachings of the popes and Vatican II to church information:

> Man's right to be informed is a rational, inherent right. It is given him by God Himself. It is not a privilege conferred by any authority. Any agencies, then, that utilize the media are bound to do so in a way that respects this right, be those agencies ecclesial or civil. If there have been abuses of this right by any authorities in the Church, we members of the People of God can only regretfully acknowledge the fact and at the same time strive to amend our ways.

In the discussions leading to the American bishops' landmark decision in November 1971 to open their future meetings to the press and other observers, three different committees of bishops issued significant reports reasoning in favor of openness.

These developments culminated in the 20,000-word Pastoral Instruction from the Pontifical Commission for the Means of Social Communication, of which American Archbishop Martin O'Connor was president, and Archbishop Philip Hannan of New Orleans a member. Pope Paul VI confirmed the statement and ordered it to be published on May 23, 1971. The document summarized many of the above points about privacy and social information. In a detailed discussion of communication within the church it urged authorities to "ensure that there is responsible exchange of freely held and expressed opinion." As for information, the Pastoral Instruction stated that normal life and smooth government in the church require

> . . . a steady two-way flow of information between the ecclesiastical authorities at all levels and the faithful, as individuals and as organized groups. . . . On those occasions when the affairs of the Church require secrecy, the rules normal in civil affairs equally apply. . . . When ecclesiastical authorities are unwilling to give information, or are unable to do so, then rumor is unloosed and rumor is not a bearer of the truth but carries dangerous half-truths. Secrecy should therefore be restricted to matters that involve

the good name of individuals or that touch upon the rights of people, whether singly or collectively.

With this, the most advanced official recognition of the right to information in the church, the practice of secrecy has been faced and conquered in a surprisingly short span of years—in theory, at least. There is a sound theological basis for the church's evolving new policy on information, as well as practical reasons. But as Part I described, the church is ambivalent about the right to know. Words in decrees are subject to interpretation, and they are not always applied, particularly when entrenched ways of doing things or the personal inclinations of church leaders pull in the opposite direction. Dramatic improvements have been made in the past decade. The challenge the church faces is to take its excellent words off paper and put them fully into practice.

12 The Press and the Prelates

Early in 1973 Pope Paul VI spoke in Vatican City to a group of 200 foreign correspondents and their wives. In the course of his remarks the pontiff listed the steps that the Vatican had taken to help reporters in church coverage. But he made it clear that Catholicism has no plans to reveal everything about its affairs:

> Clearly there remain limits demanded by discretion and the common good, in the Church more than in other societies. The reason is simple. If the Church must have a good knowledge of the world she must care for, and if she must arouse broad cooperation from her children, her decisions are based upon the Gospel and her own living Tradition, not on the world's spirit nor on public opinion, which often fails to grasp the complexity of the theological or pastoral problems at stake.

The communications-minded popes, Pius, John, and Paul, have all issued cautionary statements about secular press coverage of religion. Past papal statements about the Catholic press often have been even more restrictive, describing a loyalist role that most secular newsmen would find oppressive. The height of this mentality came with Pope Leo XIII's message to the American church in 1895. Leo said that Catholic journalists, whether they worked in the church or the secular media, should unite to defend Catholicism, and should not presume to question official actions, since the bishops, "placed in the lofty position of authority, are to be obeyed." The attitude has improved under the last three popes, but they have often cautioned the Catholic press not to rock the boat. Pope John XXIII told a group of Catholic journalists that their work should be "substantially different" from operations done out of "transitory interests or by purely human cleverness," and that they should avoid polemics which do not set an example of charity or serve the Catholic community.

Pope Paul has complained repeatedly about press treatment of church controversies. In a speech to the international press union in 1968 he granted the Catholic papers' duty to report on internal controversies, but said they should not emphasize opinions opposed to church tradition which could confuse "the immense mass of the good faithful." At a meeting with the Pontifical Commission two months before it issued the important Pastoral Instruction of 1971, Paul criticized groups which use the media to divide Catholicism "by their dissemination of news of a corrosive and protesting nature." He warned that those responsible for Catholic media must reflect on any attitudes which would cause damage, for which they must render an account, not so much to the church as to God. The Pastoral Instruction cautioned that news which touches "fundamental Christian principles" should be interpreted in accordance with church teaching. Official newspapers should "try to explain fully the thinking of the organization for which they are accepted as public spokesmen." On the other hand, the document takes a fairly liberal view on the free expression of various ideas within the church.

The Pastoral Instruction stated:

> Since the development of public opinion within the Church is essential, individual Catholics have the right to all the information they need to play their active role in the life of the Church. In practice this means that communications media must be available for the task. These should not only exist in sufficient number but also reach all the People of God. Where necessary, they may even be owned by the Church as long as they truly fulfill their purpose. . . . [The Catholic press] must also achieve professional

standards in printing up-to-date, accurate and comprehensive news about
the life of the Church. . . . It is hard to see how people can keep in touch
with what is happening in the Church without the Catholic press.

Catholic newspapering in America began with the founding of the
United States Catholic Miscellany by Bishop England of Charleston,
South Carolina, in 1822. In the century and a half since, the Catholic
press has grown to an impressive network of 140 newspapers with 5.4
million readers, plus a plethora of magazines with 16 million subscribers. Although a few bishops and a number of priests were involved in the pioneering days, most of the Catholic press was operated
and edited by laymen. This period featured such fearless journalists
as Orestes Brownson and Isaac Hecker, whose concept of freedom of
information was more advanced than that of many Catholic journalists even today. In the nineteenth century, says Monsignor Vincent
Yzermans, "bishops vocally attacked fellow bishops; priests in print
violently disagreed with bishops; laymen publicly and openly differed
with pastors and bishops. To read these papers today makes our
present communications endeavors seem to appear as no more than
polite, tea-party versions of the virility of Catholicism."

In the immigrant days the Catholic press had the major task of
guarding the faith and the church against calumnies from the Protestant majority. Prelates such as Archbishop John Hughes of New York
began worrying that the church would be identified with the controversial opinions of lay editors. In a pastoral letter in 1866 the American
hierarchy emphasized the distinction between official teaching and lay
editors' opinions, in the course of making generally friendly remarks
about the Catholic press. The bishops said a paper was a diocesan
"organ" only in the sense that it was the outlet which the bishop used
occasionally to print official documents. But relations between the
editors and the bishops deteriorated. The economic depression of 1893
forced many lay editors to bow out, and papers eventually came under
direct episcopal control. Pope Leo XIII's 1899 encyclical attacking the
"Americanist" heresy had a repressive impact.

Yzermans says the diocesan press as it exists today was consol-
idated roughly between 1910 and 1930. The result was the medieval-
style "controlled press," reflecting "ecclesiastical adolescence" and
"Catholic paranoia." Yzermans recalls that someone once counted 13
photos of Cardinal Spellman in one 16-page tabloid edition of New
York's *Catholic News.* A sadly revealing document from this era was
a 1939 book called *Swim—or Sink,* which contained testimonials on
the Catholic press from 93 American bishops. Most of them asserted
that the press' role was to protect the faith against such enemies as
secular morality and Communism. The bishop who headed the national press department, John Mark Gannon, maintained that "the
Catholic Church must take care of itself." Others used the vocabulary
of combat, referred to the evils of Spain's secular press, and called the
press a "watchdog," even a "mouthpiece" for the pope. The entire
book contained virtually nothing about the press' responsibility to
inform church members. Yzermans believes that "since the diocesan
press has been almost totally taken over by the bishops, the church
has suffered a great deal through unconsciously stifling the voice of
public opinion in the church." And, he points out, it is the whole
people of God, not the bishops, who pay for the publication of the
papers.

In the years since World War II the diocesan press has shown
somewhat more independence, particularly with the advent of Vatican Council II, and the National Catholic News Service, which operates under the wing of the U.S. hierarchy, has improved markedly in
candor and initiative. But these changes have not been without ten-
sions, and many observers sense a retrenchment in the past few years.

In the era of Vatican II, many reformist writers have emphasized
the Catholic press' duty to inform its readers. In *The De-Romanization
of the American Catholic Church* (1966) priest-sociologist Joseph
Scheuer and former newsman Edward Wakin cited several case studies of important church stories that had been played down or ignored
in the Catholic press. The result, they said, was that "today the best
and most reliable coverage of major Catholic news often appears in

non-Catholic publications," and church members have been forced to get information from these outside media. One of the more pungent items in this literature was the chapter on the press in *The People Versus Rome* (1969) by John O'Connor, the diocesan editor in Wilmington, Delaware, who was forced out of his job in a dispute with his bishop. O'Connor said that in the years since Pius XII first advocated public opinion in the church,

> precious little has been done to advance the development of an informed, participating people, while so much is still being done to throttle the four freedoms necessary for a vigorous and viable public opinion: freedom of inquiry, freedom of information, freedom of discussion, and freedom of expression. The obstacles to a healthy development are a controlled press, unaccountable officials, and, saddest of all but a direct result of the first two, a people conditioned to shrugging apathy.

The reform writers such as O'Connor give much heavier emphasis to the related problem of censorship than to open information, an issue on which Catholic editors have been remarkably quiet. For the more liberal elements, getting antiestablishment commentary out in the open evidently is more important than the dissemination of hard information. The present book has sidestepped the censorship debate because there is so much material available on this question, and so little on secrecy. The two are related, since censorship is one of the tools that is used to protect secrets. But secrecy is not inextricably linked to censorship. For instance, the Southern Baptists practiced some censorship recently by scuttling a commentary on Genesis put out by the denominational press because it was too liberal. But there was no secrecy about the contested ideas, which were thrashed out before thousands of persons in an open convention. In the Catholic context secrecy and censorship merge when the media seek to report on new theological speculations and the hierarchy tries to suppress both the ideas and the attendant publicity. Although Catholic censorship was established to perpetuate doctrinal purity, it seems to be waning fast for that purpose even while it persists as a shield for church administration.

The broad question of the limits on church-owned publications is not so simple as it might seem to some secular journalists. It might well be legitimate for a church paper to be more restrictive on pastoral and personal matters, or on elemental morals and doctrine, than on the coverage of policy and administration. To take an extreme example, what if a writer for a diocesan weekly wants to write an article proposing that America's racial problems be "solved" by exporting all Blacks to Africa by force? The bishop would be within his rights to decide that such an idea violates Christian teaching, and to censor publication on grounds of conscience. Such internal limits on the freedom to publish seem particularly defensible in a society where the bishops have no monopoly on the publication of ideas, and where there are ample outlets in independent Catholic and secular publications. Part of the meaning of freedom is the freedom of Catholics to own a newspaper and refuse to promote in its pages the idea that baptism should follow a personal decision of faith, or the idea that the Eucharist is merely symbolic—and the freedom of Baptists to print just the opposite.

However, the episcopal veto should be used very sparingly and is inexcusable on matters of mere administrative policy. When the bishop entwines the editor in the middle of the bureaucracy, the results are journalistically grim. The best way for officialdom to set policy limits for church papers is to choose an editor who honestly agrees with the basic religious beliefs that the paper stands for, and then to turn him loose to do with the paper what he wants, even when it hurts.

As for the special problem of reporting controversial theological ideas, Catholic editors often have had to ignore major news stories such as the theologians' protest against Pope Paul's birth control encyclical, to avoid "scandalizing the faithful." The sensible policy in such cases would be to run a fair "hard news" account of who is saying what. If the newspaper wishes, it can then knock down the ideas in an editorial or column. If the bishop attacks the ideas, that is legitimate news and should also be covered. This approach apparently is hard to adjust to because in the more monolithic past even the news columns were considered an arm of the church's teaching authority, so that news articles constituted advocacy of ideas rather than the mere reporting that some persons hold these ideas. The option of ignoring controversial ideas in news coverage makes little sense because they will be exposed in independent Catholic and secular media anyway.

The past emphasis on opinion rather than on fact has had a negative influence on the Catholic press. Thomas Stritch, the communications chairman at Notre Dame, theorized that the popularity of columnists has encouraged "the younger men and women to think in terms of editorials, comment and exhortation, instead of reporting. Catholic journalism has largely ignored the *Time*-inspired team journalism, with its emphasis on dramatic fact backed by research." Commentary, which ought to be the dessert of journalism, has become the main course.

The results of this showed up in a poll of the reading habits of 500 diocesan priests, published in the February 1972 *U.S. Catholic*. The poll indicated a move away from the traditional idea of the Catholic press as an arm or teaching tool of the hierarchy. But when asked to rank five functions of the church press, the priests put the informing of members far below the evaluation of secular events and serving as a forum for new ideas. Oddly enough, the liberal priests, who supposedly favor the "forum" idea, saw little value in the competitive nature of the Catholic press. They seemed to expect the entire press to turn liberal. Conservatives proved far more willing to read liberal Catholic papers than the liberals were to read conservative papers. In the light of Stritch's remark it is interesting that besides local papers, only two publications with a "very high" intensity of readership were read by at least half of the priests polled: *Time* (read by 71.9 per cent), and *The National Catholic Reporter* (read by 62.8 per cent).

This high ranking for the *Reporter* shows the significance of the independent Catholic publications in the modern church. The pioneer on the left was *Commonweal* magazine, while *The Wanderer* has anchored the right wing for years. The conservatives, well-funded by razor-blade magnate Patrick Frawley, have been on the rise in recent years. To complete with the *Reporter* in the newspaper field, they established *Twin Circle* and later bought out *The National Catholic Register.* In the same period *Our Sunday Visitor* moved rightward again, and these three weeklies combined swamp the *Reporter's* circulation. Although the *Reporter* and *Commonweal* retain more influence with key priests than do the conservative newspapers, the conservative bloc has also gained a clergy foothold with the purchase of the venerable *Homiletic and Pastoral Review.*

The independent press provides an interesting counterpoint to the omissions of the official church press. In Protestantism, for example, there was a time when the denominational magazines were in conservative hands. In those days the liberal *Christian Century* arose to fill a crucial place in dispensing information and opinion. More recently the church-run press has tended to be the outlet for a liberal establishment, neglecting news and opinion of interest to moderate Evangelicals and the right-wingers. So conservatives at the grass roots have been forced to create new publications without denominational subsidies, some of which are thriving even as the official publications decline. Some are interdenominational, others aim at particular denominations or groups of denominations. The same phenomenon has occurred in Sunday school and book publishing. We can also see the beginnings of a party system in Catholic publishing. In the continuing competition of freely expressed news and opinion—a natural result of the growing pluralism in most church bodies—all parties benefit.

When it comes to reporting Catholic news, the lay-edited *National Catholic Reporter,* whatever its future holds, has already won a place in church history for its founder, Robert Hoyt. The paper began as a spinoff of the Kansas City diocesan weekly in 1964, with an assist from Bishop Charles Helmsing. Since then its great independence and initiative in covering the postconciliar church have created unprecedented controversies. An outstanding example was its publication of the pro-contraception report by the majority of Pope Paul's advisers before he issued his anti-contraception decree. The *Reporter*'s greatness came from its news and information. It also offered liberal opinion pieces, but so did *Commonweal,* the more saucy magazine *The Critic,* and other publications. Despite the consternation caused by the *Reporter*'s various scoops, the paper came under bitter condemnation from Helmsing and the Vatican, not for its news coverage, but for questioning traditional dogma. The underlying issue of information has thus been obscured in the controversy over the newspaper.

Partly as a result of the *Reporter* debate the Catholic Press Association and the American bishops began a dialogue on the role of the church press. The papers from a study session of editors and bishops in 1969 contain surprisingly little about the information problem. But some valuable comments were provided by noted Jesuit theologian Walter Burghardt in his paper, "Toward a Theology of the Press." Burghardt said that the principle, "better ignorance than confusion," was widespread in the hierarchy. In fact, he cautioned, with today's mass media there is little likelihood of sheer ignorance. People will learn some things, so the choice is between partial and inaccurate knowledge, and full knowledge. With the need for church public opinion, he said, "the primary function of the Catholic press is to supply the people with the material, the information, which will make it possible for them to have informed opinions." Rather than presenting the one, proper Catholic opinion in an editorial, the editor should provide the background and documentation which make informed discussion possible. A statement of consensus from the meeting said that the Catholic press enlightens the church "by informing and instructing its readers" (presumably on church affairs as well as on external events, although this was not specified). Both editor and bishop, the conference said, "should recognize that the right to information is a right of the reader which should not be abridged. Reporting news involves good news and bad, joys and sorrows, order and disorder."

Another, more bleak prospectus was provided by John Deedy in the *New Catholic Encyclopedia.* He said the church press faced a possible future "heavy with duties but shut off from the right that is basic to proper functioning: the right to the facts at their source and as they are, not as someone in whatever position of authority chooses to make, unmake, or withhold them." He said Catholic papers need little hierarchical supervision because they practice "self-censorship," instinctively presenting to readers "as much or as little as the establishment wishes."

It seems an open question whether church leaders or the mass church membership desire a vigorous press. There has been a grim roll call of publications shutting down, and of leading editors leaving in disillusionment. Hoyt, who personified an era, was ousted in a palace coup by *Reporter* Publisher Donald Thorman, who is trying to keep up the investigative reporting but with a more irenic tone to keep the newspaper alive. *Ramparts* remained identifiably Catholic for only a brief while, and even *Commonweal* now appears embarrassed to be too "Catholic." For all publications, rising costs shadow the future, and Yzermans thinks consolidation into statewide newspapers will be necessary for survival.

The diocesan press will continue to depend on church subsidies, and unless the bishops commit themselves to a free press, the Catholic papers will be trapped between episcopal pressures and secular competition. If the Catholic newspapers are not essential sources of information, the competition from the improving coverage in the secular press could prove ruinous.

Widespread and professional-quality news coverage of Catholicism and other religions in America is a relatively recent development.

Although *Time* magazine has had a Religion section from its first issue in 1923, the modern age in newspaper coverage dates roughly from 1949 and the founding of the Religion Newswriters Association for specialists in the field working for the secular press in the U.S. and Canada. During Vatican II many of the smaller papers came to realize that religion is legitimate news, not just a matter of listing speakers and socials. Paul Williams, who led the *Sun* newspapers' investigative team on the Boys Town finances, neatly summarized this attitude in a statement issued when the papers won the first extraordinary citation ever awarded by the R.N.A.:

> If we are to continue to have a free press in a free society, that press must meet a special, unique obligation. It must report fully and fairly on the institutions of that society. I am talking about *all* of the institutions: government at all levels, business, education, and your special field of religion. If we want people to understand what's happening in America today, we have to tell them how things work. Not how the institutions *say* things work. Not even how their leaders *want* them to work or originally intended them to work. But how they *actually* work.

As "hard news" and investigative reporting in religion improves, the secular press is also expanding into broader conceptual areas that were once the preserve of the church press. At the same time, religion reporters are faced with competition from a bewildering variety of new religious groups and gurus. For some, institutional problems are boring, and for most, such stories are only part of the task. The religion reporter today must analyze the movements and moods, both within the mainstream churches and outside of them.

Although bishops sometimes complain about anti-Catholic bias in the media, the opposite side of the coin is episcopal news management, not only through controlling what information is released, but by informally pressuring secular editors. Symptoms of this disease were the complaints about protection of Catholicism by top editors that came from Betty Medsger when she left the *Philadelphia Bulletin* and

R.N.A. President William Folger when he resigned from the *Buffalo Courier-Express*. Similar charges have been made privately by other reporters about the newspapers where they are still employed.

The most-publicized case involved Janice Law of the *Houston Chronicle*. She was forced off the paper after a bitter exchange with her editors over being required to run a retraction on her story about priests leaving the church. It turned out that the "facts" for the retraction had been supplied by the diocesan chancellor, Bernard Ganter (now a bishop), to the newspaper's city editor, Zarko Franks. And Franks had complained about Mrs. Law's tough Catholic coverage before he had been promoted to city editor. The R.N.A. ordered a local investigation of the fuss, which was inconclusive, and then sent in Stanford Communications Professor William Rivers to prepare a report. Rivers concluded that church pressure, in effect, had led to the dismissal of a good reporter, and that in major facts at issue Mrs. Law was right and the chancellor was wrong.

Such horror stories, once commonplace, now stand out because of their rarity. Pressure on secular media is unusual if only because it seldom works. Most secular reporters have the independence to follow the news wherever it leads them. The arena of significant conflict is the Catholic press, which exists in the no-man's-land between independent journalism and the interests of the institutional church. The future fortunes of the Catholic press will indicate to the world whether the official policy on freedom of information described in Chapter 11 is genuine.

13 Some Protestant Secrets

Not many reporters cover the conventions of the Gideons, the hotel-Bible people. But that was my first major assignment when I left general newspaper work and began specializing in religious news for *Christianity Today* magazine. The news edge for the piece turned out to be that the Gideons were no longer just in the hotel business. That year they planned to place 1.3 million King James Version New Testaments in the nation's public schoolrooms. The Gideons' president, a lawyer who had fought unsuccessfully against a New Jersey court ruling that such placements were unconstitutional, pleaded with me not to mention the school project. It would "close the doors" and "harm the Lord's work," he explained.

That was the first time I started thinking about Christian candor and news coverage. Since the magazine for which I was writing was sympathetic to the Gideons' cause, I immediately raised the objection with my boss, the then News Editor David E. Kucharsky. His reply: "The work of the sort of God who is revealed to us in the Bible is not going to be harmed, in the long run, by telling the truth to the public." The story ran with a school Bible lead.

The Evangelical Protestant publications like *Christianity Today* are significant in comparison with the Catholic press, because both are trying to rise above the "ghetto" mentality of the past, and because both hold to a series of normative religious beliefs. The Evangelicals have been wary of reporters and other outsiders, because—like the Catholic immigrants—they were on the cultural margin for a long time. This started sometime after the Scopes Trial, and ended sometime before Billy Graham began preaching at the White House. As for beliefs, it was argued above that church-owned papers have a right to control the publication of ideas that are offensive to the owners. (This refers to the endorsement of ideas, not the factual coverage of the news, however embarrassing.) In many Protestant groups in North America the list of theological and moral certainties has been shrinking all the time, which eliminates the whole censorship problem. Although *Time* got a lot of criticism from pious subscribers over its famous "Is God Dead?" cover story, that question had been raised originally in the Protestant prints. Catholics and Evangelicals, however, operate a press with theological limits.

Have these limits affected Evangelical news coverage? The Evangelical newsman's dilemma was stated succinctly by the Rev. Dr. J. D. Douglas, a silver-penned Scot, in a paper prepared for a Graham-sponsored writing school in Australia. At some point the newsman "must make a choice between suppressing the facts in the name of Christian charity, and reporting them in the name of journalistic integrity." The Graham association's British wing purchased *The Christian,* a century-old British Evangelical weekly, and later hired Douglas as its editor, then shut the paper down for good in 1969. The ostensible reason for the execution was the paper's budget deficit, but since it had been subsidized for years there was every reason to believe that the real cause of death was *The Christian*'s candid comment and news coverage of Evangelical foibles.

The editor of Graham's major publication, *Decision* magazine, the Rev. Dr. Sherwood Wirt, complained about the negativism he saw creeping into the Evangelical press and proposed a "new note" in religious journalism. Writing in *Christianity Today,* he said "if we can't write a constructive report on a church activity perhaps we shouldn't write about it at all." Another well-known Evangelical journalist, Jim Johnson, responded that Wirt's note is nothing new. "It has, in fact, been the one ingredient that has too often stifled honest reporting within the church, for too long a time," causing Evangelicalism to languish under "sham, hypocrisy, and a sterile and withered outreach." Fortunately, as the Evangelicals have gained in self-confidence, their candor quotient has been rising, with investigative reports on conservative embarrassments in *Christianity Today* and *Eternity.* Sharp commentary is coming from a series of small new publications such as the *Post-American, Inside, The Other Side, The Wittenberg Door,* and some of the Jesus Movement papers such as *Right On.*

What is the attitude of Protestant officialdom toward freedom of information? It is easy to describe Catholic policy and teaching, but difficult to generalize about the attitude in the hundreds of Protestant denominations and para-church organizations. Examples of secrecy practices in some of the important groups follow.

The World Council of Churches is the rough Protestant-Orthodox equivalent of the Vatican, and it practices somewhat more secrecy than its U.S. constituency does. Its occasional big Assemblies are open, but they have a relatively small role in determining the program. The 120-member Central Committee, with representatives from around the globe, meets about once a year and holds occasional closed sessions, although the practice is not abused. However, the small Executive Committee which confers several times a year to supervise the ongoing program meets entirely in secret. When the W.C.C. executive conferred in New Zealand in 1972, the nation's press was disappointed to find it could not cover the discussions. The *Star* in New Zealand's largest city, Christchurch, editorialized that people of all religions, or none, would be "both astonished and disappointed" by the W.C.C. policy. "It should be a great occasion when world church leaders visit this country. Their views and the decisions of the church body on so many contentious issues should be given the widest publicity so that people can understand not only what is being done, but the reasons for it."

The United Methodist Church's Council of Bishops has always met secretly, except for some special open hearings. After the Catholic bishops opened up, the Methodist bishops also relented, but only part way. During a five-day meeting in 1973 they opened one afternoon session to the press and to anyone else who could fit in the observers' gallery. This secrecy is inexcusable, but it has not caused much of an uproar because Methodist policies are set by the General Conference and the national program is enacted by the staff. The bishops have considerable power within their own jurisdictions, but as a group they have little authority. Secrecy in official meetings becomes crucial when the meetings have the power to set policy.

Before he became the editor of the *Christian Century,* the Rev. James M. Wall crusaded for openness as editor of the official magazine for Methodist ministers, the *Christian Advocate.* He wrote an editorial lament when the commission working on a new structure for national agencies held an entire two-day meeting in executive session and excluded reporters. Wall said the church at large has no "need to know" such things as why a bishop reassigns a particular pastor. But the restructure affected the whole church. Wall confessed that the Protestant press has been "too guilty in the last decade of allowing the 'official' church to set the pace for what was news within the church. We need to be much more candid and open in the coverage of church news."

Wall also campaigned for candor in the campaigning before episcopal elections. Like many groups, Methodism operates under the myth that the office seeks out the reluctant servant of God through the unaided operation of the Holy Spirit, as ballots are cast. In fact, said Wall, the vote is preceded by game-playing, vote-trading, sly grins, awkward meetings, and well-scripted speaking trips. He favors open campaigning, formal nominating speeches, and open balloting. "We must choose leaders who can exercise authority and we must do so with maximum involvement of those over whom the authority is to be exercised."

U.S. Lutherans have been demythologizing their elections. The

American Lutheran Church chose the late Dr. Kent Knutson as president after its first open campaign with stated nominees in advance of the convention, and with no great loss of spirituality. The Lutheran Church—Missouri Synod has been forced out of its old ways by an internal civil war between two organized theological parties, one moderately conservative and the other committed to total orthodoxy and Biblical literalism. The orthodox leader, Dr. Jacob A. O. Preus, managed to defeat a moderate incumbent as church president in 1969 under the traditional system that prevented open campaigning or even formal nominations. But in the 1973 election (which Preus won handily) each congregation had the power to nominate a candidate. For the first time the vote totals on the convention balloting, as well as the congregational nominations, were announced publicly.

As Preus has clamped down on doctrine the news reports on controversies have mostly disappeared from the official church press and have been forced into various opinionated independent publications. At the height of the furor the official editorial commission decreed that it would "terminate discussion of controversial matters related to the St. Louis seminary" in the church press and leave the debating to local and regional meetings. In the same period Indiana District President E. H. Zimmermann presented an amazing and lengthy report to the council of district presidents, complaining about press handling of the doctrinal battle. He maintained that the moderates had no right "to carry the internal problems of the Church to the secular press. . . . We cannot prevent secular writers from saying what they want to say, but we can avoid feeding the secular press articles and information that create confusion, unrest and division. We can avoid going to the public press with matters that only the Church understands, and that can only be resolved by the Church." To Preus' credit, the denominational headquarters sent out press releases on major statements from the anti-Preus movement, as well as from his supporters, in the months before the presidential election.

Three months after the Missouri Synod Lutherans, the Episcopal

Church's General Convention elected a new Presiding Bishop, John M. Allin of Mississippi, to a twelve-year term. The election in Louisville was historic because the House of Bishops for the first time released the names of the three nominating committee choices and the men who had been nominated from the floor, two days before the vote. The bishops' election itself was behind locked doors, as usual, but afterward for the first time the vote totals for each candidate on each ballot were announced. The other half of the bicameral General Convention, the House of Deputies (lower clergy and laity), held fast to its traditions, however. It has the duty of voting to endorse the bishops' selection, and this is done in secret. The approval had always been a mere formality, but in Louisville one-third of the deputies responded to liberal fears and voted for an extraordinary consultation with the bishops over whether Allin was acceptable. This discussion was highly important for the denomination, and of course all the details leaked out quickly, but the deputies insisted on secrecy. Presumably the purpose of the secrecy was to protect the individual involved, but the objections to Allin were not personal embarrassments but questions of policy.

In Canada the bishops of the Anglican Church traditionally have met in secret. Except when it votes for the Presiding Bishop, the U.S. House of Bishops holds open meetings, but it often slips conveniently into executive session and dismisses outsiders when something touchy arises. One bishop remarked enigmatically, "Tongue cannot tell, nor mind comprehend, what goes on in some of those sessions."

At the 1970 General Convention some reporters were interested in how various regions of the country had voted on the touchy question of ordaining women. But officials hustled the press out of the ballot-counting room because such breakdowns of the vote are secret. No one is supposed to know how a particular diocese votes on any question unless the delegates themselves order a roll call. Reporters' appeals to the president of the house, noted New York rector John Coburn, were to no avail.

Under Allin's predecessor, John Hines, the Episcopal Church faced questions of financial accountability in the conduct of the General Convention Special Program, which granted millions of dollars to minority-group organizations working for political and economic power. For instance, when Malcolm X Liberation University in North Carolina asked for $75,000 on top of an original grant of $45,000, local Episcopalians complained that they had been unable to get necessary information about the project from the denominational staff. Malcolm X's director Howard Fuller then withdrew the fund request, explaining "our operations are always open to the observation of Black people. . . . Our efforts are not secret; they are simply not open to white people's investigation and participation." Wall Street's wealthy Trinity Episcopal Church is just as secretive, refusing to reveal the value of its real estate holdings (estimated by the *New York Times* at $47.7 million) or of its fabled stock portfolio.

The Southern Baptist Convention, which has become the biggest U.S. Protestant body, is one of the more candid denominations. Like Catholicism, the Southern Baptists have produced a lively network of state newspapers. The *Baptist Standard* in Texas, which has the biggest circulation of any newspaper in the state, is a powerful voice when it comments on Baptist or state issues. The S.B.C. constitution establishes an information department with the specified duty of informing both members and outsiders. Reporters often find out about Baptist controversies first, rather than last, in articles released by the denomination's Baptist Press service at Nashville headquarters, e.g., the lamentable decision to refuse Blacks membership at the First Baptist Church of Birmingham, Alabama. Doctrinal traditionalism, a trait which is generally shared by Southern Baptists and Catholics, does not automatically produce secrecy.

But the Southern Baptists have had their problems. In 1970 the executive board of the Arkansas state convention decided to admit reporters only "on invitation." A subsequent survey discovered that all other state boards and most national S.B.C. agencies had an official policy of open meetings. Baptist Press, the denominational news service, has bypassed at least three controversies until they could not be ignored: the conservative opposition to a church press commentary on Genesis, the same agency's decision to scuttle a teen-agers' magazine that showed a Black boy talking to two white girls, and a financial scandal in Missouri. The Missouri case involved the late Earl Harding, who developed considerable power among the pastors in the state during his many years as executive secretary of the state convention. (Which brings to mind a story from former Congressman Brooks Hays, who served as S.B.C. president. It involved a Baptist who converted to the Episcopal Church on his deathbed. The reason: "I want to be in a church where the bishops are *visible.*") Harding had floated an interest-free loan of $62,500 for his own home from convention funds, and secret expenses of $53,150 in 1971 were unaccounted for. In 1973 laymen forced the executive committee to open up and authorize an audit. Baptist Press limped in with a story two weeks after the *St. Louis Post-Dispatch.* Even though Baptist Press only hinted at the scandal, Harding sought to intimidate the denominational press, and it was two months before Baptist Press carried a full story on the situation. Jim Newton, the excellent reporter who was the B.P. news editor at the time, remarked, "Ultimately secrecy never works—the truth always comes out. Harding would have been smarter to say 'I've got nothing to hide.' "

Robert Hastings, editor of the *Illinois Baptist,* wrote on an earlier dispute that "a private corporation, operated for profit, has a right to discuss its business in private. But a Baptist deliberative body is not for profit and it does not ordinarily earn its own funds. Although there are exceptions, the money comes from the free-will gifts of the rank-and-file Baptists in the pews." Hastings argued that if church officials "are above board, they should welcome inquiry and the full sharing of information. An open press is the best friend that a conscientious church leader can have. In that open press, the issues will be aired and debated until truth eventually comes to the front."

In the United Presbyterian Church a recent rabble-rouser on

secrecy was the Rev. Dennis Shoemaker, co-editor of an adult education magazine. He took to the pages of the *Christian Century* to complain about the brutal firing of headquarters staff made necessary by a financial pinch. Shoemaker's own magazine ran an all-out defense of homosexuality as "neither sin nor sickness" without suffering any censorship. (Speaking of censorship, it is interesting that in an entire issue Shoemaker did not include a single article in favor of the traditional Christian teaching against the practice of homosexuality.) The trouble came with a fierce article from a women's liberationist who said that the church was so sexist that libbers must either destroy it or leave it. Officials censored the article, which led Shoemaker to conclude that the church press "isn't free when the preservation of the institutional church is the issue at stake."

In another instance Shoemaker wanted to run a thorough report on an organization in Colombia which was aided by denominational mission funds. The problem was that the group engaged in violence, although the church aimed its money at its nonviolent activities. Shoemaker figured that with an article explaining that this violence resulted from prior terrorism inflicted on the people aided by the project, and that the people had little choice but to fight for survival, Presbyterians would back the idea. But the article was never written and the denomination put out "vague and misleading" information, according to Shoemaker, fearing that if the story became known it "could destroy financial support for this and other mission projects." So the membership learned about the project from a polemical account in a conservative Presbyterian newspaper.

In the U.S. the Eastern Orthodox communions typically hold three types of meetings. There are national conventions, open to all church members and the public, that discuss church issues but do not act on them. Meetings of the bishops, and of policy-making councils that include priests and the laity, are customarily secret. Elsewhere, most of the affairs of Orthodoxy usually are conducted behind closed doors. In 1972 dissidents in the Orthodox Church of Greece protested plans to hold a meeting of the hierarchy which was not only secret but was to have a special rule forbidding any bishop to talk to the press afterward. This obviously weakened the hand of the dissidents, who opposed the primate installed under the heavy influence of the nation's military junta.

America's esoteric religions, which tend to be highly undemocratic and to fear hostility from outsiders, are often very secretive. Such groups as the Jehovah's Witnesses, the Black Muslims, and Eastern religions are overt about seeking converts, but keep a tight lid on their internal affairs. In Herbert W. Armstrong's Worldwide Church of God, until a policy change in 1973 only fully indoctrinated members were admitted to church services, which usually were held anonymously in rented halls. Churches and ministers were never even listed in the Yellow Pages. Christian Science, a much more established group, is one of the few religions that refuses to report even the number of adherents. Financial facts are also concealed from the membership by the self-perpetuating five-member board that controls church affairs. (For other aspects of the closed system, see Charles Braden, *Christian Science Today*.) Money has always been a mystery in the major Utah branch of the Latter-Day Saints (Mormons). In 1972 the church lifted the veil a bit by announcing that it had spent $17.7 million in the previous year in its welfare program for needy members. The report, which told nothing about the total church financial picture, was aimed at a Salt Lake County proposal to tax the welfare system, which includes farms, factories, and canneries. The church does pay taxes on the many nonreligious businesses it owns, such as a hotel, newspaper, TV station, and department stores. The Temple rites of the Mormons are among the most tightly guarded religious exercises in the West.

Secrecy is one of the traits that distinguishes the eccentric Children of God from the mainstream of the Jesus People movement. An article in *Christianity Today* accused C.O.G. leader David "Moses" Berg of "unconscionable duplicity" by quoting what the Children are told to say for public consumption and what they practice in their inner circles. A flier for outsiders claimed "nothing is kept hidden or secret" but the Children advocate the "Selah treatment," or sweet-talking of inquirers. A leadership manual said "honesty is *usually* the best policy" with the press, but advised later on, "you can just stall, evade, or lead them off on another track." Since the Children are forbidden to hold paying jobs, "procurers" go around asking for donations, and they often cover up the fact that they are part of the controversial Children.

Generally, when a mainstream Protestant bureaucrat is found practicing secrecy, it is with a sheepish grin on his face, rather than with the righteous visage of the secretive Catholic prelate. In the major Protestant denominations many of the crucial policy debates occur in the privacy of agency offices, or in the relatively private sessions of small executive boards which include elected representatives. The major national conventions that the press covers are often places where previous practices and budgets are ratified with minimal debate. There is little doubt that some programs are initiated consciously without prior disclosure to reduce opposition from the grass roots. But at least the Protestants have the structure for public debates in their top-level legislatures, and such debates arise eventually on most major issues. Most of the Protestant bodies file regular, public reports on finances and program, and they generally practice a fairly high degree of internal democracy—with the information flow that accompanies it, from the parish level on up.

Secrecy is one of those subtle differences in style that have begun to be an issue as ecumenism has gone beyond the superficial stage. The U.S. Catholic bishops rankled some Protestants with a secret 1968 directive on the official theological talks with various denominations. The statement said that notice of meetings should be released only after they have been held, and should report only the general topic of the discussion, not the substance. This unrealistic policy has faded in practice.

With Vatican II's decree on ecumenism the Catholic church is freer to examine the information practices of the "separated brethren" and to consider whether they might be worthwhile for itself. Protestants, despite their more open style, would benefit from studying and taking seriously the Catholic theological rationale for candor, described in earlier chapters, since they persist in some secrecy.

14 Prospects for an Open Church

Secrecy can hardly be considered a Christian atmosphere for the conduct of human affairs in society, much less in the church. In ecclesiastical history the growth of secrecy represented a drift away from the precedents established in the New Testament and the early centuries, largely from outside influences. The descent into secrecy in the Catholic church was largely a modern development, culminating in the dismal administrative style of the last century. Catholicism has always stressed privacy (or secrecy) in personal and pastoral matters because of its healthy theological respect for the individual, but this same principle requires openness, rather than secrecy, in the conduct of institutions.

The Catholic church generally has been more secretive than Protestantism, but in recent years it has applied its previous recognition of the people's right to information squarely to the administration of the church itself. Despite this new theoretical justification for candor and some commendable changes in practice, particularly in the United States, Catholicism remains ambivalent about freedom of information in the church. Since there are good theological and practical reasons for openness, and yet secrecy persists, obviously there are other factors against change. What are some of these other influences, how seriously do they darken the prospects for an open church, and what might overcome them?

Paradoxically, some of the liberals who desire Catholic reform may unwittingly undercut the cause of freedom of information. They seek to dilute the authority of church teaching when it now provides ample backing for freedom of information. Some downgrade the authority and reliability of the New Testament, which offers the earliest and most important example of the open church. Others erode the basis upon which ethical demands can be made of the church by questioning the existence of natural law, or by undermining absolutes in moral theology such as truthtelling. Finally, some despair of the institutional church at the very moment when that institution is undergoing creative reappraisal.

Beyond the normal tendency of officials to protect information that might undercut their authority, moralist Daniel Maguire observes another phenomenon. He argues that all governments depend on secrecy to perpetuate a sense of mystery and thus enhance their power. The perpetuation of the myths requires secrecy, and secrecy aids in the concentration of power. Normally, officials do not cede power voluntarily. Maguire thinks this is the basic reason for the secrecy practices of the Catholic hierarchy. Yet in describing the church in Holland, journalist John Horgan says that it has removed the mystery of the *hierarchy* without impairing the mystery of the *church.*

The majority of the hierarchy is also convinced that openness aids the dissidents in the church. In general, this is true. Jean Cardinal Danielou epitomized this mindset when he told a conservative journalist, "There has been a crisis in the exercise of authority because a small group of theologians and journalists have been terrorizing the bishops." The danger in this attitude is that the dissidents might well turn out to be right on a particular issue, as they often have in Catholic history. The competing theory is that with free information and opinion, the truth will triumph in the long run. This *laissez-faire* attitude once got the young church out of a good deal of trouble. When Peter and the other apostolic leaders were brought before the Sanhedrin in

Jerusalem, Rabbi Gamaliel urged caution in how they were treated. He ran through a list of false leaders who eventually had been discredited without repression, then concluded:

"Leave these men alone and let them go. If this enterprise, this movement of theirs, is of human origin it will break up of its own accord; but if it does in fact come from God you will not only be unable to destroy them, but you might find yourselves fighting against God" (Acts 5:38, 39).

True enough, Catholic dissent is usually associated with church "liberals." Many of the writers cited in this book in favor of freedom of information come from the liberal side. But as the church evolves, there could come a time when publicity and openness would protect the interests of a conservative minority. Since traditionalists generally control the hierarchy today, they have come under attack on the secrecy issue. But as Francis X. Murphy observed a few years ago, "when the tables are turned, those in power will continue to protect their interests," and he doubts that the liberals would prove paragons of virtue in providing free information. Religion reporters have been amused to note the secrecy in meetings of some liberal clergy and lay caucuses—from the very groups that have attacked the insularity of the hierarchy.

Gerald Renner blamed the secrecy of the hierarchy on "an illusion that anything less than a façade of unanimity in all matters would 'scandalize the faithful.' This illusion was rooted in an immigrant church where 'Father knew best.' " Former Bishop James Shannon recalled that in reporting to the press during bishops' meetings, he was under pressure to play down differences:

There was an unspoken assumption that the bishops are always unanimous. Often no poll was taken, and I couldn't report the existence of dissent. It was an unhealthy sign for a body of alert men drawn from across a continent. In fact, those differences were signs of the church's strength, not its weakness. In the process, the people and the public at large lost the voice of the far-thinking bishops who expressed minority opinions. I recall a pastoral letter in which men who sought to return to the lay status were called "derelict priests." Some of the bishops pleaded that this be taken out because it was not a fair characterization of all of these men. When the statement came out, that phrase drew fire. It would have helped if the public knew that some bishops also took exception to it.

Another explanation for secrecy is plain inertia. The concept of free church information is quite new, and the church is led by older men who worked for decades under the old secrecy system. For some of them, change is fearful, or impossible. In *The Pope and the Press* (1968) Hugh Morley stated the same point in institutional terms. All complex organizations, he wrote, have a tendency to become more complex, cumbersome, cluttered, and inefficient, and to stray from their original sense of purpose. Catholicism is one of the biggest, and one of the oldest. Along the same line, Shannon remarked that "secrecy is ingrained in every large organization—big corporations, universities, churches. Particularly if they are not sure what is sensitive and what is not, they decide, 'Let's just put the cover over it.' In the church, leaders have followed the unspoken premise that 'we're doing the work of God; we don't *have* to communicate.' "

Some attribute the secretiveness to a particular psychology ingrained in the Catholic priesthood. In the past priests have been trained in isolation. Until the 1950s many seminaries forbade students to read daily newspapers. Yzermans says that the clergy are "the most incompetent of all critics of the press. Priests, generally, because of their training, expect newspapers to carry propaganda items; but to the good newsman, propaganda is nothing more than cheap advertising. Most clerics, in my experience, condemn the press for the wrong reasons. If a church official complains about the press, the first presumption is that he himself has not been open and honest with the press. This is not to say that newsmen do not make mistakes. It is merely to state the case that newsmen only make mistakes when the sources of information are closed to them and they have to revert to the 'jungle telegraph' system of reporting." Beyond the particular issue of the press, priests have often shown evidence of an ingrown clerical culture, feeling more comfortable in the company of other priests than of laymen, except the old-fashioned, subservient kind. Some observers have psychologized about a ghetto priesthood which fears the "outside world."

But Benjamin Schneider of the University of Maryland and Douglas T. Hall of York University, Ontario, put the blame on the system. The two men did an intensive study of the priestly career system, at the invitation of the Archdiocese of Hartford. Schneider said, "The term secrecy attributes it somehow to the individual priest. Our view of the Catholic organization is that it lacks opportunities for participation by those who would contribute something. Whoever is in the top position assumes it's *his* decision to make, in fact his obligation, due to the position he's in. He doesn't think to consult with anyone else. It's just not done in that system."

The intensive Hall-Schneider research in Hartford described an employment system, now starting to improve, which traditionally has reinforced insecurity and inertia among priests. The institution overshadows personal choices. "There is little evidence of active choosing on the part of the priest, and little evidence of the system offering any opportunity to choose." "One is hard-pressed to think of extant occupational systems of professional personnel with fewer structural opportunities for psychological success and growth." The priest in this archdiocese typically languished 22 years before getting his own parish, had no choice over the type or place of asssignment, no choice in living arrangements, found success difficult to define or measure, and felt he was underutilized. It will be difficult to extend co-responsibility in church government to the laity until all segments of the clergy are co-responsible. As this changes, so will the psychology of priests, and of the bishops who rise from the priestly ranks.

Whatever the reasons for continuing secretiveness, and despite recent indications of a retrenchment in church reform, the pressures in favor of freedom of information should prove stronger in the long run. Openness increases respect for Catholicism in the broader society, and enhances the influence of the faith. The church not only needs to avoid the appearance of hypocrisy by putting its own stated principles into practice, but it faces a situation in which the very health of the institution requires freedom of information. In an anti-institutional age, the institution of the church must do all it can to enchance its own grass-roots support through credibility and accountability. In the wake of Watergate and Vietnam, the public will use higher standards in judging the candor of officialdom. Besides distrust of institutions, many younger people are no longer interested in them. Despite all the supposed allure of mystery, the church is most likely to remain interesting to the mass of the public if it is open and forthright.

Another factor in change is the assimilation of U.S. Catholic culture. The Catholic population was once a compact, definable entity within America. Each wave of immigrants lived in Catholic neighborhoods in the cities, and was vitally interested in the church. Then the group gradually filtered throughout the society. The Catholic church will remain robust only if it is attractive, institutionally and spiritually, as this cultural function declines. Freedom of information is one factor that will help. Besides this, assimilation will increase the influence of alternative lifestyles within the Catholic membership, particularly democratic secular government and, in an ecumenical age, the practices of Protestants.

Some forecasters go further than this, and argue that church authority is in great trouble unless it makes major structural changes. Andrew M. Greeley, who directed the first major sociological study of priests ever commissioned by the U.S. bishops, drew some startling conclusions at a meeting with a committee of bishops in February 1972. Greeley said his research found a breakdown of confidence in the wisdom of church authority. "Many priests under 40 no longer believe a thing that the collective hierarchy says." Without change, "by 1980 there will be no such thing as ecclesiastical authority in the

American Church (except over the checkbook)" and those bishops who overcome the skepticism of priests will have done so by their own efforts. Greeley proposed representative government to overcome this authority problem, including the nomination of bishops by priests. "There is no way short of it for the leadership to regain the power it has lost." Greeley contended that the current "cronyism" in the choice of church leaders so discredits the hierarchy that eventually it will be unable to govern. The system of choosing bishops is likely to become a crucial issue in American Catholicism.

While the election of bishops would doubtless enhance freedom of information, openness should also flourish if the present system continues. No matter how they are chosen, the leaders of the people of God are accountable to those people. This link is part of successful human governance in the very "nature of things," and it is the only approach that fulfills the intent of Scripture and theology. It is also, of course, a style in harmony with the American culture within which the church must live.

Perhaps the most important influence will be the revival of the laity that was envisioned by Vatican II. For many years the hierarchy purposely kept information from the membership. The old-style layman was a spiritual child, and the clergy commitment to Catholicism became almost a surrogate for lay commitment. As Morley commented, the hierarchy—like a parent who fails to communicate with his child—insulted intelligence and alienated respect. The modern layman must be an informed layman, and this must not mean selective information trickling down from on high, but complete two-way communication. Freedom of information will never come about solely through officials sitting in chancery offices and agreeing that they will not have any more secrets. The full freedom will come when the secular press, the Catholic press, the laity, and the general public insist on their right to know.

Selected Bibliography

BOOKS

Ambrosini, Maria Luisa, with Mary Willis. *The Secret Archives of the Vatican*. Boston: Little, Brown, 1969.

Barnds, William J., *et al. The Right to Know to Withhold & to Lie*. New York: Council on Religion and International Affairs, 1969.

Bingham, Joseph. *The Antiquities of the Christian Church*. London: Henry G. Bohn, 1856.

Brown, William E., and Greeley, Andrew M. *Can Catholic Schools Survive?* New York: Sheed and Ward, 1970.

Callahan, Daniel. *Honesty in the Church*. New York: Scribner's, 1965.

Congar, Yves M. J. *Lay People in the Church*. Westminster, Md.: Newman, 1965.

Cross, Harold L. *The People's Right to Know*. New York: Columbia University, 1953.

Ernst, Morris L., and Schwartz, Alan U.. *Privacy*. New York: Macmillan, 1962.

Gollin, James. *Worldly Goods*. New York: Random House, 1971. (Thorough study of Catholic finances.)

Hall, Douglas T., and Schneider, Benjamin. *The Working Lives of Priests*. New York: Seminar Press, 1972. (Intensive survey of the Archdiocese of Hartford.)

Häring, Bernard. *The Law of Christ*. Westminster, Md.: Newman, 1966.

Hatch, Edwin. *The Organization of the Early Christian Churches*. London: Longmans, Green, 1918.

169

Heston, Edward L. *The Press and Vatican II.* South Bend: University of Notre Dame, 1967.

Kaiser, Robert Blair. *Pope, Council and World.* New York: Macmillan, 1963.

Küng, Hans. *Structures of the Church.* South Bend: University of Notre Dame, 1968.

———. *Truthfulness.* New York: Sheed and Ward, 1968.

Lo Bello, Nino. *The Vatican Empire.* New York: Trident, 1968.

———. *Vatican, U.S.A.* New York: Trident, 1972.

McGurn, Barrett. *A Reporter Looks at the Vatican.* New York: Coward-McCann, 1962.

McKenzie, John L. *Authority in the Church.* New York: Sheed and Ward, 1966.

Miller, Arthur R. *The Assault on Privacy.* Ann Arbor: University of Michigan, 1971.

Moran, William. *The Government of the Church in the First Century.* New York: Benziger Bros., 1913.

Morley, Hugh. *The Pope and the Press.* South Bend: University of Notre Dame, 1968. (On Pope Paul VI.)

Pember, Don R. *Privacy and the Press.* Seattle: University of Washington, 1972.

Rahner, Karl. *Free Speech in the Church.* New York: Sheed and Ward, 1959.

Rourke, Francis E. *Secrecy and Publicity.* Baltimore: Johns Hopkins, 1961.

Tiemann, William. *The Right to Silence: Privileged Communication and the Pastor.* Richmond: John Knox, 1964. (Protestant view.)

Tournier, Paul. *Secrets.* Richmond: John Knox, 1965.

Turberville, A. S. *Medieval Heresy and the Inquisition.* London: Crosby Lockwood & Son, 1920.

Westin, Alan F. *Privacy and Freedom.* New York: Atheneum, 1968.

Whalen, William. *Christianity and American Freemasonry.* Milwaukee: Bruce, 1958.

Wiggins, James Russell. *Freedom or Secrecy.* New York: Oxford, 1964.

Wise, David. *The Politics of Lying.* New York: Random House, 1973.

Yzermans, Vincent A. *Valiant Heralds of Truth.* Westminster, Md.: Newman, 1958. (Pope Pius XII on communications.)

OTHER

Beaufort, L. J. "Freedom of Information," *Catholic Mind,* September 1948, 545–551.

Gabel, Emile. "Freedom of Information," *America,* August 10, 1963, 133–135.

Lee, John A. "The Communication of the Roman Catholic Church to the World, 1968–1970," Ph.D. dissertation, University of Minnesota, 1970.

Martin-Descaloza, Jose Luis. "The Problems Raised by the Communication of Religious Matters and Information About the Church," lecture at Seminar on Morals and the Mass Media, Holy Cross Abbey, Madrid, September 1969.

Morley, Hugh. "Role of Church and State in Human Right to Information," *Catholic Messenger* (Davenport, Iowa), February 4, 1965, 5.

Pontifical Commission for the Means of Social Communication. "Pastoral Instruction for the Application of the Decree of the Second Vatican Ecumenical Council on the Means of Social Communication," Washington, D.C.: U.S. Catholic Conference, 1971.

Acknowledgments

Many persons have contributed to this book. The scholars whose writings proved particularly valuable have been mentioned by name. Two former information directors for the U.S. Catholic bishops, Monsignor Vincent Yzermans and Gerald Renner, were particularly helpful. Many of my friends in the Religion Newswriters Association shared their experiences with me. For general background, the comprehensive daily dispatches of Religious News Service, New York City, proved invaluable. My wife Joan provided many important suggestions as the manuscript was in progress. Some sources of information will remain anonymous.

The historical and theoretical research began with a thesis written in conjunction with an M.A. in Religion from The George Washington University in September 1970. Warm appreciation is extended to my thesis adviser, the Rev. Dr. Harry E. Yeide, Jr., the members of the religion faculty, and the university.

Scripture quotations are from *The Jerusalem Bible* (Garden City, N.Y.: Doubleday, 1966).